ALFRED'S BASIC
Electronic Keyboard Course

FOR INSTRUMENTS WITH AUTOMATIC RHYTHMS AND "SINGLE-FINGER" CHORDS

Willard A. Palmer ■ *Morton Manus* ■ *Amanda Vick Lethco*

FOREWORD

Today's ELECTRONIC KEYBOARDS are among the wonders of modern technology. At the touch of a button they can provide rhythms for all types of music, whether it be swing, rock, disco, waltz, Latin music—just about anything. Playing one key can produce a full chord of three or more notes. Other features provide a running accompaniment of broken chords or variations that fit perfectly with the harmony. The bass patterns are also automatically generated, and they often seem to sense exactly the right notes to accompany the melody you are playing with the right hand. A choice of various instrumental effects is also available, such as piano, flute, guitar, organ and many others. Some instruments even provide keys that light up to help you find certain keys to press. All of these features add up to fun and excitement, and they can make learning to play an exciting experience. But to play well on these instruments you need to know more than previously published teaching aids have provided.

This book, designed for use with any electronic keyboard with 44 or more keys and automatic chord and rhythm effects, is unique in that it not only teaches how to use these features and to understand what they do, but also how to read music in treble and bass clefs, like a professional. With this book you can also learn to form "fingered chords" (combining three or more notes yourself) with left and right hand. Everything is so clearly explained that this book can be used as a method for self-instruction. It will also serve as an excellent and thorough introduction to keyboard playing for those desiring to move on to larger instruments, with or without automatic features, such as piano, organ or synthesizer.

This book progresses very smoothly, with no gaps that might tempt the student to skip over hard sections. The entire presentation can be completed in a surprisingly short time, after which the student should be able to move on to standard sheet music and play popular songs. The familiar favorites and tuneful original pieces in this book will add to the fun and enjoyment of learning, and will lead to the rewards of competent musicianship.

2

CONTENTS

Position at the Keyboard

Metal or wooden stands are available as accessories for many keyboards. These stands hold the instrument in the correct playing position, so the surface of the keys is 27 to 30 inches from the floor.

If you can not obtain a stand for your instrument, a desk or table will do.

Good posture at the keyboard makes playing easier. Sit squarely in front of the keyboard, and observe the following points:

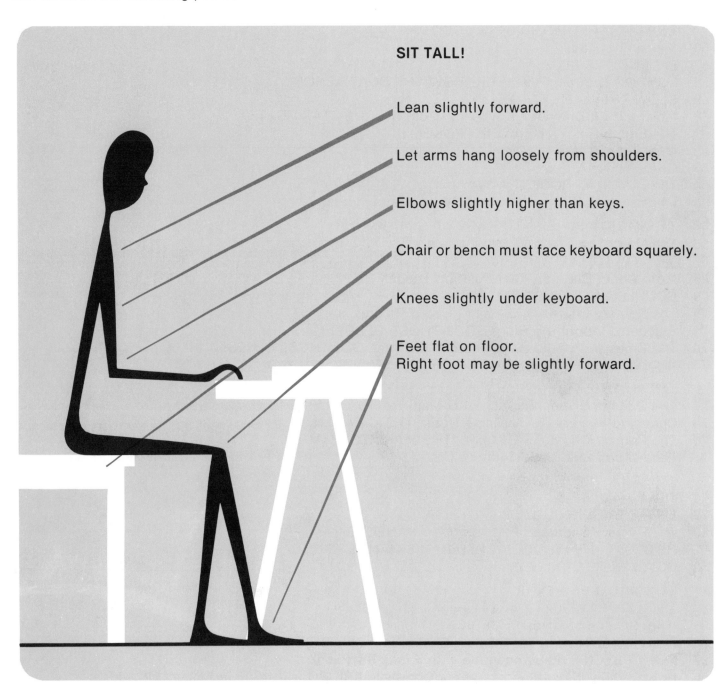

SIT TALL!

Lean slightly forward.

Let arms hang loosely from shoulders.

Elbows slightly higher than keys.

Chair or bench must face keyboard squarely.

Knees slightly under keyboard.

Feet flat on floor.
Right foot may be slightly forward.

About Music Racks or Holders

Most instruments have a music rack, but a few small table-top instruments do not. You can improvise a holder for your music books by using an easel-type picture frame on the table behind your instrument, or you can tape a piece of heavy cardboard on the back of your instrument, with an easel-type flap attached to hold it at the proper angle.

Finger Numbers

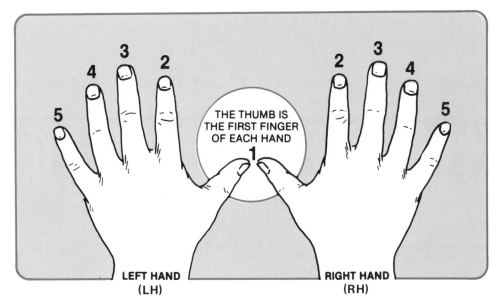

THE THUMB IS THE FIRST FINGER OF EACH HAND

LEFT HAND
(LH)

RIGHT HAND
(RH)

Response to reading finger numbers should be automatic. Before you begin to play, practice moving each finger as you say its number aloud.

Curve your fingers when you play!

Pretend you have a bubble in your hand.

Hold the bubble gently, so it doesn't break!

Preparing to Play

1. Turn power on.
2. Your instrument has an AUTOMATIC CHORD feature, called by various names on different instruments (often just the brand name plus the word "CHORD"). See your owner's manual. In this book we refer to it as "Auto." Turn it OFF for the present.
3. Your instrument has a number of PRESET SOUNDS or VOICE SELECTORS. These are named for various instruments, such as PIANO, ORGAN, GUITAR, etc. In this book we will usually indicate which ones to use. They will be designated by the word "Register."
4. Your instrument also has a RHYTHM section. It provides drum beats and also causes the chords of the Auto feature to play in rhythm. This section is controlled by START and STOP buttons. On many instruments, the two are combined in one START/STOP button. If Rhythm begins to play when it is not needed, press the STOP button.
5. Adjust the MASTER or MAIN VOLUME control to any level you choose.

Ready to Begin

Auto: OFF   **Rhythm:** OFF   **Register:** PIANO

1. Play ANY WHITE KEY with the 2nd finger of the RH (right hand). BE SURE TO CURVE YOUR FINGERS!
2. Play several more with the same hand. Play the keys with just enough pressure to produce a sound.
3. Play several more white keys, using the 2nd finger of the LH (left hand).
4. Repeat the above several times, using a different Register each time. Listen to the different sounds you can create.

The Keyboard

The keyboard is made up of white keys and black keys.
The black keys are in groups of 2's and 3's.

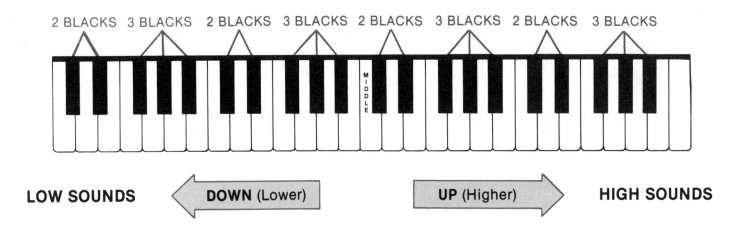

On the keyboard, DOWN is to the LEFT, and UP is to the RIGHT.
As you move LEFT, the tones sound LOWER. As you move RIGHT, the tones sound HIGHER.

Play the 2 BLACK KEY groups!   Auto: OFF   Rhythm: OFF   Register: PIANO

1. Using L H 2 3, begin at the middle and play all the 2 black key groups going ◁ DOWN the keyboard (both keys at once).

2. Using R H 2 3, begin at the middle and play all the 2 black key groups going UP ▷ the keyboard (both keys at once).

Play the 3 BLACK KEY groups!

3. Using L H 2 3 4, begin at the middle and play all the 3 black key groups going ◁ DOWN the keyboard (all 3 keys at once).

4. Using R H 2 3 4, begin at the middle and play all the 3 black key groups going UP ▷ the keyboard (all 3 keys at once).

Using the SUSTAIN Feature

The SUSTAIN button causes the tones to linger after you have released the keys.

1. Using the PIANO Register with Sustain OFF, play all the 2 black key groups, ONE KEY AT A TIME, using LH 2 3 going DOWN the keyboard. Play again with Sustain ON. Listen to the difference!

2. Using the PIANO Register with Sustain OFF, play all the 3 black key groups, ONE KEY AT A TIME, using RH 2 3 4 going UP the keyboard. Play again with Sustain ON. Listen to the difference!

3. Repeat all of the above, using the ORGAN Register, first with Sustain OFF, then with Sustain ON. Try other Registers. On some instruments the difference in the sustained effect on certain Registers is more pronounced than others. Listen carefully!

Name That Key!

Keys are named for the first seven letters of the alphabet, beginning with A.

A B C D E F G

Each white key is recognized by its position in or next to a black key group!

For example: **A**'s are found between the **TOP TWO KEYS** of each **3 BLACK KEY GROUP.**

Auto: OFF   **Rhythm:** OFF   **Register:** PIANO   **Sustain:** ON

Play the following. Use LH 2 for keys below the middle of the keyboard.
Use RH 2 for keys above the middle of the keyboard.

Say the name of each key aloud as you play!

Play all the A's on your keyboard.

Play all the B's.

Play all the C's.

Play all the D's.

Play all the E's.

Play all the F's.

Play all the G's.

You can now name every white key on your instrument!

The key names are **A   B   C   D   E   F   G,** used over and over!

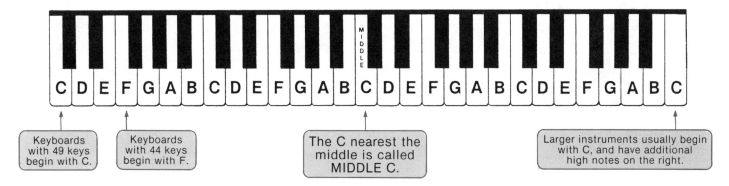

Keyboards with 49 keys begin with C.

Keyboards with 44 keys begin with F.

The C nearest the middle is called MIDDLE C.

Larger instruments usually begin with C, and have additional high notes on the right.

Going **UP** the keyboard, the notes sound **HIGHER and HIGHER!**

IMPORTANT! Play and name each white key, beginning with the lowest key (on the left).
Use LH 2 for keys below middle C, and RH 2 for keys above middle C.

Right Hand C Position

Place the RH on the keyboard so the **1st FINGER** falls on **MIDDLE C.**
Let the remaining 4 fingers fall naturally on the next 4 white keys.
Keep the fingers curved and relaxed.

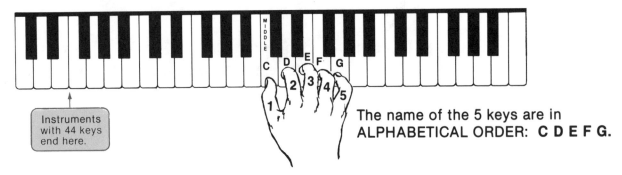

Instruments with 44 keys end here.

The name of the 5 keys are in ALPHABETICAL ORDER: **C D E F G.**

Notes for this position are written on the TREBLE STAFF.

The TREBLE STAFF has 5 lines and 4 spaces.

Middle C is written on a short line below the staff, called a *leger* line. D is written in the space below the staff. Each next higher note is written on the next higher line or space.

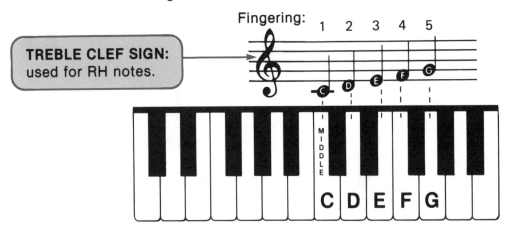

TREBLE CLEF SIGN: used for RH notes.

RIGHT HAND WARM-UP

Auto: OFF
Rhythm: OFF
Register: PIANO
Sustain: ON

Play the following *WARM-UP.* Say the name of each note aloud as you play.
Repeat until you can play smoothly and evenly. As the notes go higher on the keyboard,
they are written higher on the staff!

Fingers:

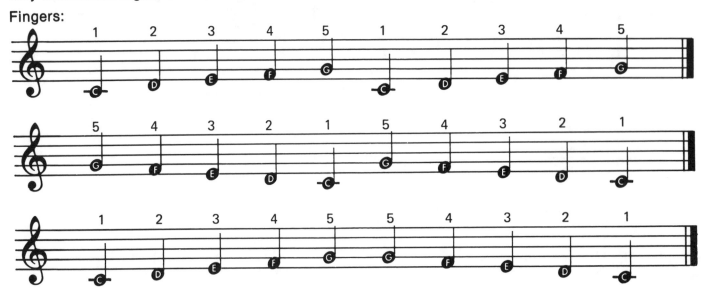

Quarter Notes & Half Notes

Music is made up of **short** tones and **long** tones. We write these tones in **notes,**
and we measure their lengths by **counting.** The combining of notes into patterns is called RHYTHM.

Clap (or tap) the following rhythm. Clap ONCE for each note, counting aloud.

Notice how the BAR LINES divide the music into MEASURES of equal duration.

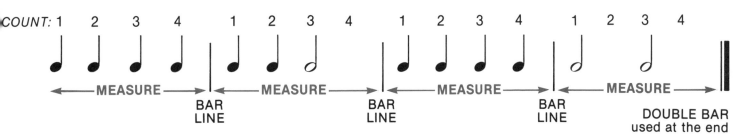

ODE TO JOY *(Theme from Beethoven's 9th Symphony)*

Auto: OFF   **Rhythm:** OFF   **Register:** ORGAN   **Sustain:** OFF

1. Clap (or tap) the rhythm evenly, counting aloud.
2. Play with RH, singing (or saying) the finger numbers.
3. Play again, counting aloud.
4. Play again, singing (or saying) the note names.
5. Play again with Sustain ON. Which do you like best with this Register?
6. Try other Registers with Sustain ON, and again with Sustain OFF.

Fingers:

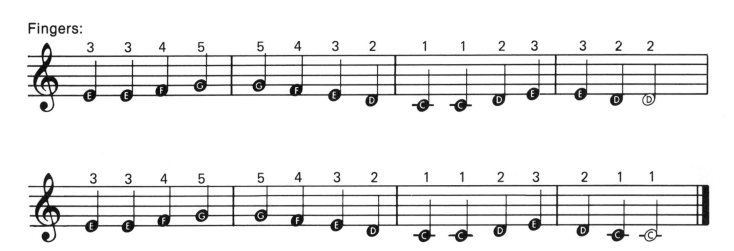

Left Hand C Position

Place the LH on the keyboard so the **5th FINGER** falls on the **C BELOW** (to the left of) **MIDDLE C.**
Let the remaining fingers fall naturally on the next 4 white keys.
Keep the fingers curved and relaxed.

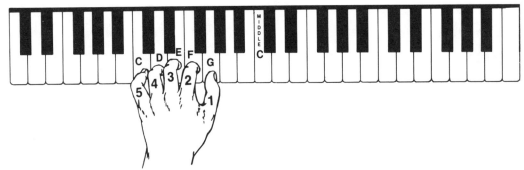

NOTES for this position are written on the BASS STAFF.

The BASS STAFF also has 5 lines and 4 spaces.
The C, played by 5, is written on the 2nd space of the staff.
Each next higher note is written on the next higher line or space.

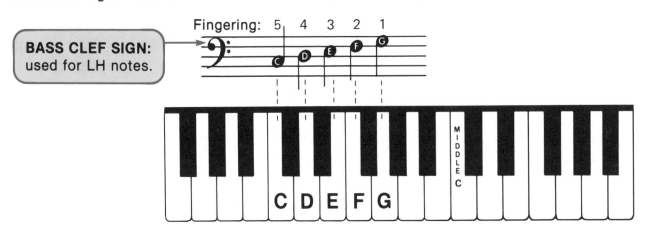

BASS CLEF SIGN: used for LH notes.

LEFT HAND WARM-UP

Auto: OFF **Register:** PIANO
Rhythm: OFF **Sustain:** ON

Play the following *WARM-UP.* Say the name of each note aloud as you play.
Repeat until you can play smoothly and evenly.

When notes are BELOW the MIDDLE LINE of the staff, the stems usually point UP.
When notes are ON or ABOVE the MIDDLE LINE, the stems usually point DOWN.

The Whole Note

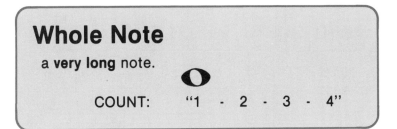

Whole Note
a **very long** note.

COUNT: "1 - 2 - 3 - 4"

Clap (or tap) the following rhythm. Clap **ONCE** for each note, counting aloud.

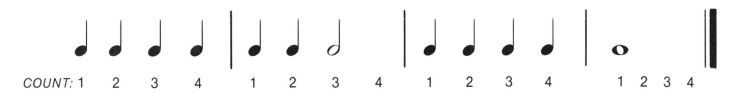

COUNT: 1 2 3 4   1 2 3 4   1 2 3 4   1 2 3 4

AURA LEE

This melody was made into a popular song, *"LOVE ME TENDER,"* sung by Elvis Presley.

Auto: OFF   **Rhythm:** OFF   **Register:** TRUMPET or ORGAN   **Sustain:** OFF

1. Clap (or tap) the rhythm, counting aloud. Count evenly.
2. Play with LH, singing (or saying) the finger numbers.
3. Play and count.
4. Play and sing (or say) the note names.
5. Play again with Sustain ON. Do you prefer this to Sustain OFF?
6. Try other Registers with Sustain OFF, and again with Sustain ON.

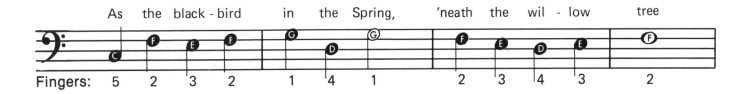

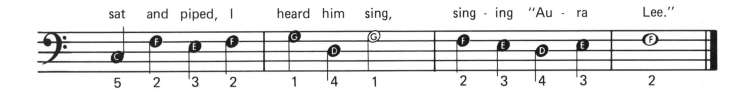

The Grand Staff

The BASS STAFF & TREBLE STAFF, when joined together with a BRACE, make up the **GRAND STAFF.**

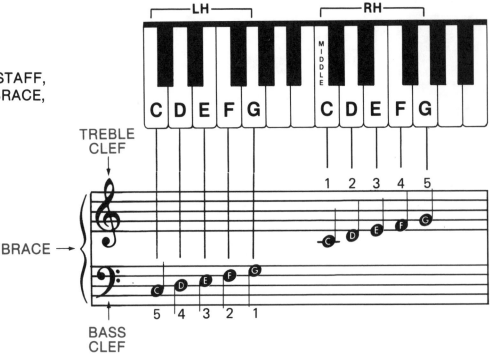

TIME SIGNATURE

Music has numbers at the beginning called the **TIME SIGNATURE.**

4 means **4** beats to each measure.

4 means a **QUARTER NOTE** ♩ gets one beat.

PLAYING ON THE GRAND STAFF

Auto: OFF   Register: PIANO
Rhythm: OFF   Sustain: ON

Only the starting finger number for each hand is given.
The following practice procedure is recommended for the rest of the pieces in this book:

1. Clap (or tap) & count.   2. Play & count.   3. Play & sing the words, if any.

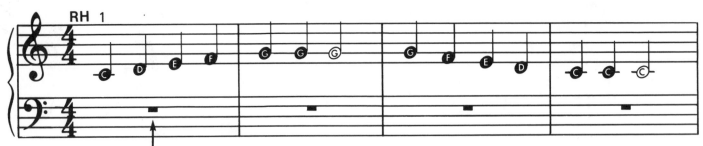

This sign ▬ is a **WHOLE REST.**
LH is silent a whole measure!

RH silent a whole measure.

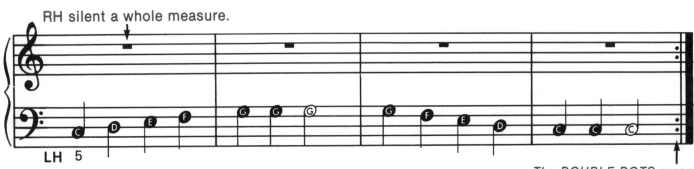

*The DOUBLE DOTS mean
REPEAT FROM THE BEGINNING.*

Rock-Along

Auto: OFF **Register:** GUITAR or PIANO
Rhythm: OFF **Sustain:** ON

Mexican Hat Dance

Auto: OFF **Register:** VIBES, PIANO or MUSIC BOX
Rhythm: OFF **Sustain:** OFF

This sign } is a **QUARTER REST.**
Rest for one count!

Adding AUTOMATIC RHYTHM

You can now add the sound of DRUMS to *ROCK-ALONG* and *MEXICAN HAT DANCE!*

The RHYTHM section is controlled by START and STOP buttons. On many instruments, this is combined in one START/STOP button.

1. Use SWING* rhythm. Turn the volume of the Rhythm section up about half-way. Press the START button.
2. The speed of the rhythmic beats is determined by the TEMPO setting. Adjust the tempo to a moderate speed by counting "1-2-3-4" and matching the tempo as nearly as you can.
3. Listen to a few measures, then play along.

*SWING is used here, rather than ROCK 'N' ROLL, because it is a simpler rhythm. Try ROCK 'N' ROLL also, if you wish.

Melodic Intervals

Distances between tones are measured in **INTERVALS**, called 2nds, 3rds, 4ths, 5ths, etc.
Notes played **SEPARATELY** make a **MELODY.**
We call the intervals between these notes **MELODIC INTERVALS.**
Notes that go up or down from a line to the next space, or from a space to the next line, move by 2nds.
Notes going from line to line or space to space move by 3rds.
Play these MELODIC 2nds & 3rds.

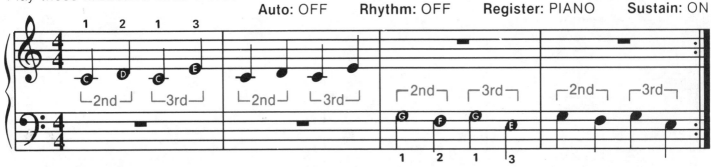

> **DYNAMIC SIGNS:** p, mf, f, tell how SOFT or LOUD to play.
> Some instruments are "touch sensitive," like a piano. When you play with more weight, the key descends faster and the tone is louder. On instruments not so equipped, you must adjust the VOLUME CONTROL before you begin to play.

AU CLAIRE DE LA LUNE

Auto: OFF   **Register:** FLUTE or PICCOLO
Rhythm: OFF   **Sustain:** OFF

> p (PIANO) = *SOFT*

TISKET, A TASKET

Auto: OFF   **Register:** BANJO or PIANO
Rhythm: OFF   **Sustain:** OFF

> mf (mezzo forte) = *MODERATELY LOUD*

OPTIONAL: Add SWING rhythm to AU CLAIRE DE LA LUNE and TISKET, A TASKET.

Harmonic Intervals

Notes played **TOGETHER** make **HARMONY**.
We call the intervals between these notes **HARMONIC INTERVALS**.

Play these HARMONIC **2nds** & **3rds**. Listen to the sound of each interval.

Auto: OFF   **Rhythm:** OFF   **Register:** PIANO   **Sustain:** ON

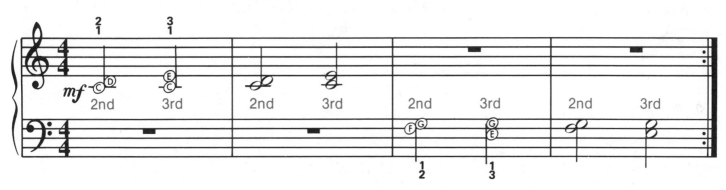

ROCKIN' INTERVALS

Auto: OFF   **Rhythm:** OFF   **Register:** PIANO, GUITAR or ORGAN   **Sustain:** OFF

Play slowly at first, counting aloud.

Quarter Rest ⁊
Rest for one count!

f (forte) = *LOUD*

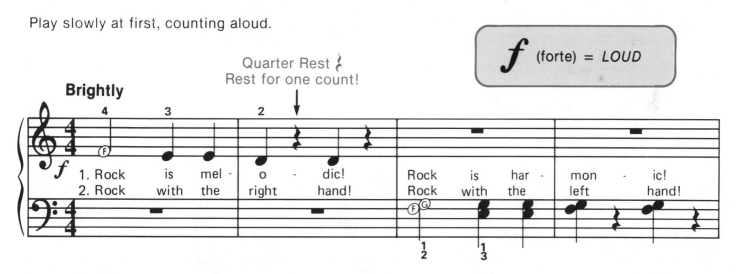

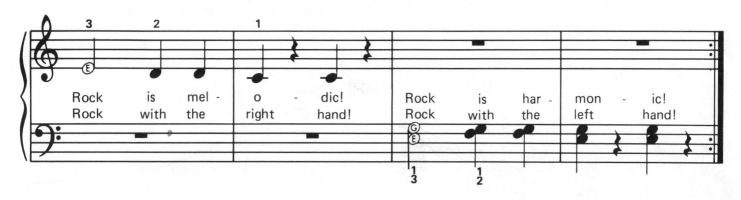

IMPORTANT! Add SWING (and/or ROCK 'N' ROLL) rhythm. Use a moderate tempo at first. Later you can play a little faster, if you wish.

Melodic 4ths & 5ths

Play these MELODIC **4ths & 5ths**.

Auto: OFF
Rhythm: OFF

Register: PIANO
Sustain: ON

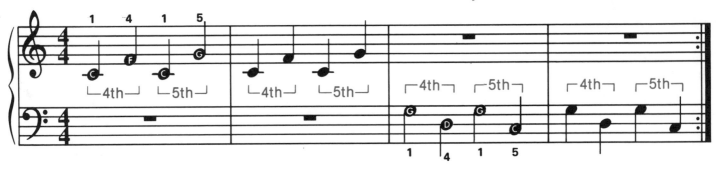

GOOD KING WENCESLAS

Find the 4ths before you play!

Auto: OFF
Rhythm: OFF

Register: VIBES, PIANO or MUSIC BOX
Sustain: ON

Moderately fast

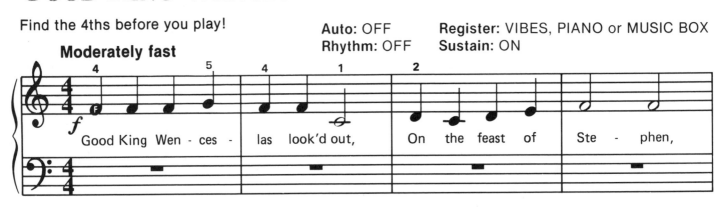

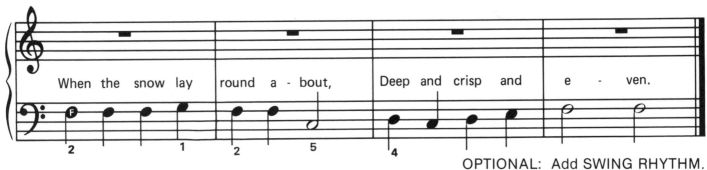

OPTIONAL: Add SWING RHYTHM.

MY FIFTH

Find the 5ths before you play!

Auto: OFF
Rhythm: OFF

Register: ORGAN or TRUMPET
Sustain: OFF

Seriously

Turn volume up on rest.

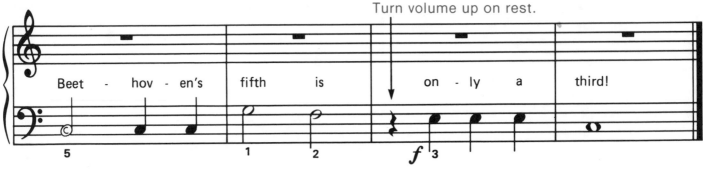

Harmonic 4ths & 5ths

Play these HARMONIC **4ths** & **5ths**.

Auto: OFF   **Register:** PIANO
Rhythm: OFF   **Sustain:** ON

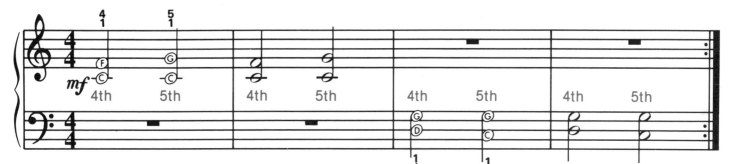

JINGLE BELLS

1. Play RH alone, then LH.
2. Play hands together.

Auto: OFF   **Register:** VIBES, PIANO or MUSIC BOX
Rhythm: OFF   **Sustain:** ON

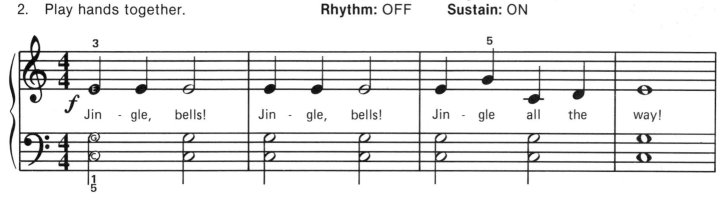

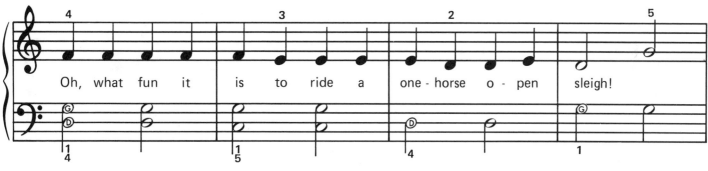

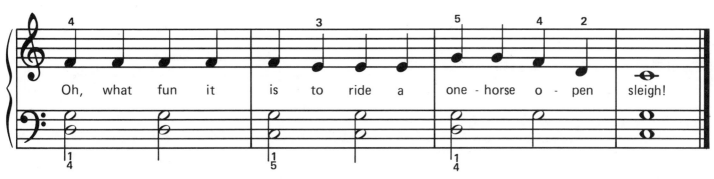

The Auto Bass Chord (Accompaniment) Section

Three or more notes played together make a CHORD. Chords are often used to provide accompaniment for melodies. Playing three-note chords requires considerable knowledge and skill. The Automatic features of your instrument will enable you to play many chords with only one finger.

The LOWEST KEYS (on the left) make up the Auto Bass Chord section (on some instruments called the CHORD or ACCOMPANIMENT section).

THE AUTO BASS CHORD (Accompaniment) SECTION

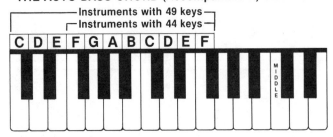

To use the automatic chords, turn the Auto control ON. Some instruments have two separate settings: "SINGLE FINGER CHORD" and "FINGERED CHORD." You will be using the "Single Finger" setting first. If your instrument has only a "Fingered Chord" setting, just turn the Auto ON, and the "Single Finger" setting will come on automatically. Consult your owner's manual, if necessary.

> By using Auto on "Single Finger" setting, any ONE key played in the *accompaniment section* will sound the three-note MAJOR CHORD of that key!

For example, to make a C MAJOR CHORD, play the single key "C" with LH 2. Play the key carefully. If you even *slightly touch* a neighboring key, a wrong chord will sound!

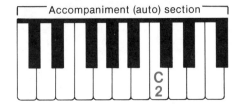

Fun with Auto ON

1. To play the following lines of music, use keys from the diagram on the right. Play each key with LH 2. The letters ABOVE the staff show which LH key to play to produce a MAJOR CHORD of the same name. Use LH 2 on each key. (This will prevent you from connecting the keys, which the instrument would interpret as playing 2 keys at once, and this would make a different chord.) Each slash-mark (✔) represents 1 count.

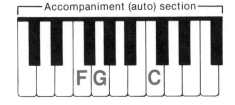

You do not have to hold each key down. Just play the key and release it. The same chord will continue to play until you touch the next LH key.

> **Auto:** ON "Single Finger"　　**Rhythm:** Moderately slow SWING
> **Register** and **Sustain:** These have no effect on the Auto section.

2. Press SYNCHRO/START, then begin. The SYNCHRO/START button "synchronizes" the rhythm with your touch, so it will start exactly when you play the first LH key.

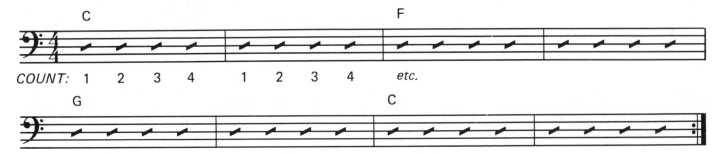

3. Using the same TEMPO setting, play the above again using other RHYTHMS. You may try all the rhythms except WALTZ. COUNT AT EXACTLY THE SAME SPEED FOR EACH RHYTHM, regardless of how many drum beats and chords you hear!

THE ONE-MAN BAND

Auto: ON "Single Finger"   **Register:** ORGAN
Rhythm: Moderately fast SWING, ROCK or SLOW ROCK   **Sustain:** OFF

1. Play RH alone, slowly, without Auto Rhythm.
2. Add Rhythm: Press START. Listen to a few measures, then play RH again.
3. Add LH: Press SYNCHRO/START, then begin. Play LH C with 2.

I'm just like a one-man band, Songs to you I bring.
I play rhy-thm, I play chords, I play ev-'ry-thing!

4. Play the above again, adding other effects, such as VARIATION, DUET, ARPEGGIO, or other features of your instrument.

   VARIATION adds different bass and rhythmic chord patterns.

   DUET adds a harmonizing note to each melody note.

   ARPEGGIO adds broken chords running up and down. On some instruments these sound automatically unless you turn the ARPEGGIO VOLUME all the way DOWN.

FOR MORE FUN: Play the exercise at the bottom of page 18 again, using SWING RHYTHM with the VARIATION or ARPEGGIO feature. Try also with other rhythms!

MUSIC WITH A BEAT

Auto: ON "Single Finger"   **Rhythm:** Moderately fast SWING   **Register:** PIANO with Sustain ON or ORGAN with Sustain OFF

1. Play RH alone, slowly, without Auto Rhythm.
2. Add Rhythm: Press START. Listen to a few measures, then play RH again.
3. Add LH: Press SYNCHRO/START, then begin. Play LH C with 2.

This sign ▬ is a HALF REST.
Rest for two counts!

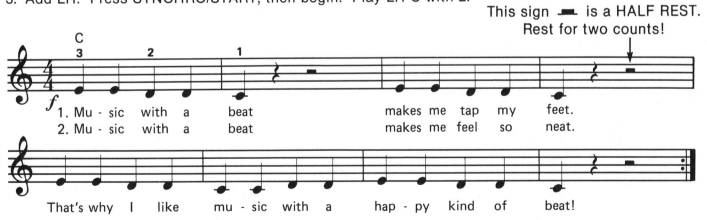

1. Mu-sic with a beat   makes me tap my feet.
2. Mu-sic with a beat   makes me feel so neat.

That's why I like mu-sic with a hap-py kind of beat!

Three Ways to END a Song

1. For a quick stop at the end, press the STOP button just after the last count.
2. To hold the last chord at the end, play the key for the last chord on the last measure of the piece. Press the STOP button with RH on the 3rd count of the last measure, while still holding the LH key.
3. FADE. Let the accompaniment continue after the piece is over, and gradually turn the MASTER VOLUME down.

Try each of these endings on the exercise on page 18, and on *ONE-MAN BAND* and *MUSIC WITH A BEAT.*

Some instruments have an ENDING button. Consult your owner's manual.

The C Major Chord

To really understand what you are doing when you play "single finger" chords, and to improve your skills as a musician, it is important that you learn to form your own chords by playing all the notes yourself, with RH as well as LH. Begin now to learn each chord as it is presented, and you will find greater enjoyment in your playing. You will also be building a good musical foundation that will enable you to move on to a larger keyboard instrument, such as a piano, organ or synthesizer.

Play this page with Auto OFF and Rhythm OFF.

The **C MAJOR CHORD** is made of three notes: **C E G.**

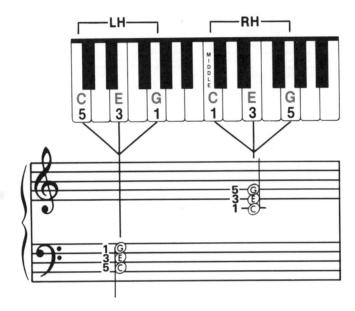

Be sure to play all three chord notes exactly together, with fingers nicely curved.

Choose any Register. Registers such as ORGAN, TRUMPET, CLARINET, VIOLIN (those named for wind instruments or bowed instruments) will sustain the chords as long as you hold the key down. Registers such as PIANO, BANJO, GUITAR, VIBES or HARPSICHORD will gradually fade away.

C MAJOR CHORDS for RH

Play & count.

C MAJOR CHORDS for LH

Play & count.

Here's a Happy Song!

Auto: OFF **Register:** PIANO
Rhythm: OFF **Sustain:** ON

READ BY PATTERNS! For LH, think:
"G, down a 2nd, down a 2nd, up a 2nd," etc.

Happily

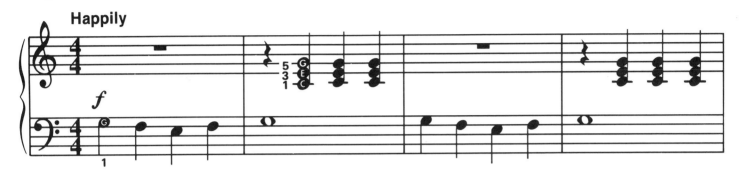

OPTIONAL: Add Rhythm. Use SWING or MARCH at a moderately slow tempo.

Brother John

Auto: OFF **Register:** ORGAN
Rhythm: OFF **Sustain:** OFF

READ BY PATTERNS! For RH, think:
"C, up a 2nd, up a 2nd, down a 3rd," etc.
THINK the pattern, then PLAY it!

Moderately fast

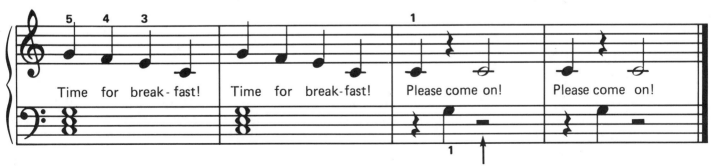

This sign ▬ is a HALF REST.
Rest for two counts!

BROTHER JOHN with Sustained Single Finger Chord

When you use the *Auto* feature without employing automatic *Rhythm,* the chords will sustain as long as you hold your finger on the key. To see how this works, play *BROTHER JOHN* as shown below.

1. Use **Auto:** ON "Single Finger"   **Rhythm:** OFF   **Register:** PIANO   **Sustain:** ON
   REMEMBER: The Register does not affect the sound of the Auto chord.

2. To play the LH chord, simply use the 2nd finger on C, as indicated by the LH note as well as the chord symbol above the treble staff. Be sure to HOLD each LH note as the whole notes indicate.

3. N.C. above the next to last measure indicates that NO CHORD is to be played. In the last two measures, simply play the LH **G** as you did on the previous page. Since this **G** is not in the ACCOMPANIMENT SECTION of your instrument, it will not sound a chord, but will play the single note **G**, exactly as before.

> IMPORTANT: To be sure the automatic Rhythm does not play,
> DO NOT press the START button, and DO NOT press SYNCHRO/START!

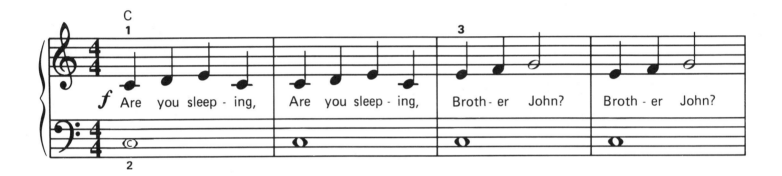

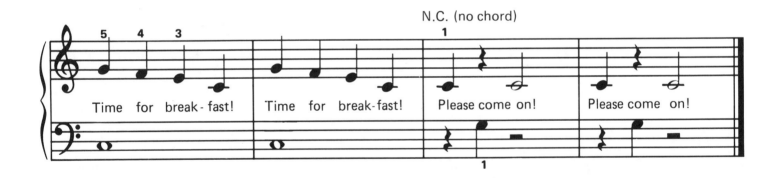

BROTHER JOHN with Rhythmic Chords

When you add automatic Rhythm to the above, you will not have to hold the LH finger on the key for the C chord to continue playing. Play *BROTHER JOHN* again, using the following setting:

Auto: ON "Single Finger"   **Rhythm:** Moderate SWING   **Register:** PIANO   **Sustain:** ON

1. Press the START button and adjust the TEMPO, counting "1-2-3-4" for a few measures. Stop the Rhythm by pressing the STOP button. Remember, some instruments combine these buttons in one START/STOP button.

2. Press SYNCHRO/START and begin. The Rhythm will begin exactly when you play the LH **C**. Do not hold the key down; just touch it at the beginning. Let it continue to play throughout the piece (in this case, even through the N.C. measures). You can play the LH **G** in the last 2 measures while the chord continues to play. This has no effect on the LH chord, because the **G** is not in the range of the accompaniment section of your instrument.

3. Play *BROTHER JOHN* again, adding VARIATION, DUET and other effects.

Introducing (B) for Left Hand

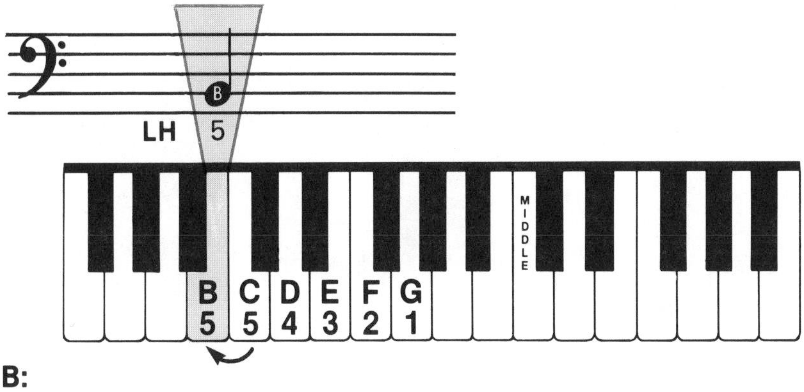

TO FIND B:

Place the LH in **C POSITION.**
Reach finger 5 one white key to the left!

Play slowly. Say the note names as you play.

Auto: OFF **Register:** PIANO
Rhythm: OFF **Sustain:** ON

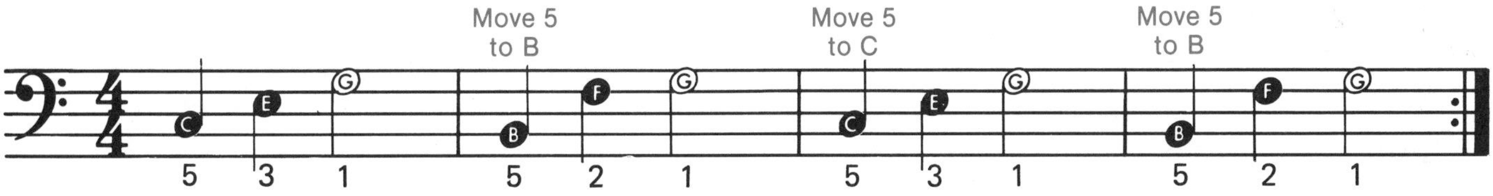

Two Important Chords

Two frequently used chords are **C MAJOR** & **G^7.**

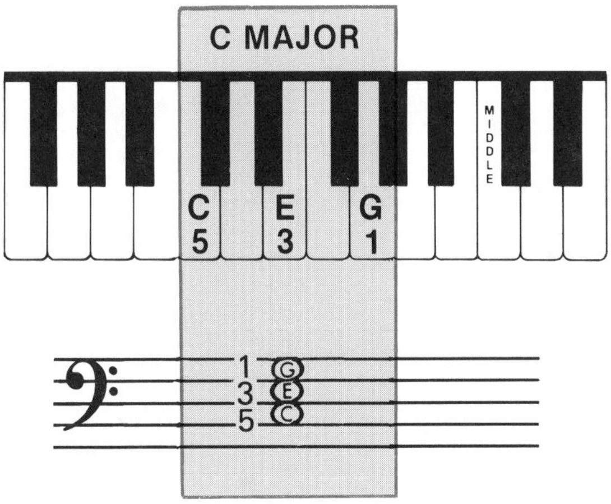

Chord symbol: **C**

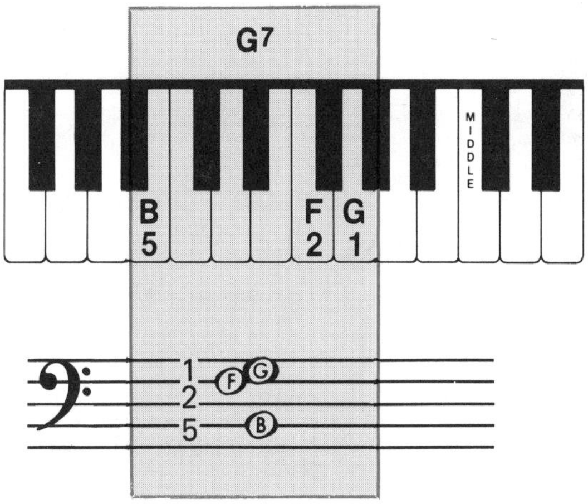

Chord symbol: **G^7**

Chord symbols are always used in popular music to identify chord names.

Practice changing from the C chord to the G^7 chord and back again:

1. The 1st finger plays G in both chords.
2. The 2nd finger plays F in the G^7 chord.
3. Only the 5th finger moves out of C POSITION (down to B) for G^7.

Auto: OFF **Rhythm:** OFF **Register:** PIANO **Sustain:** ON

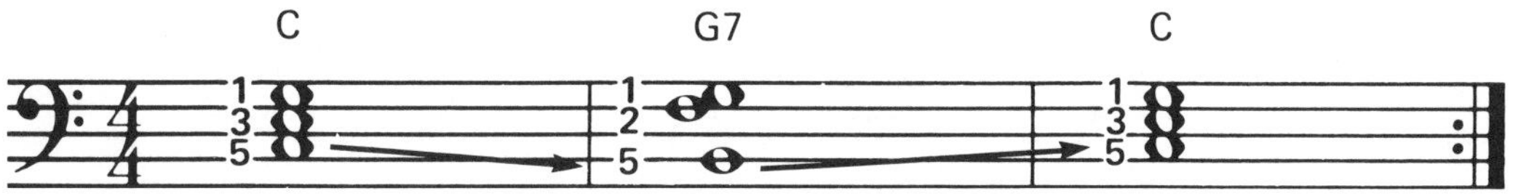

TIED NOTES: When notes on the *same* line or space are joined with a curved line, we call them **TIED NOTES.**

The key is held down for the COMBINED VALUES OF BOTH NOTES!

COUNT: "1 - 2 - 3 - 4,   1 - 2 - 3 - 4."

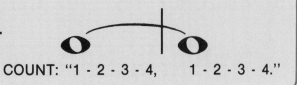

MERRILY WE ROLL ALONG

Auto: OFF   **Rhythm:** OFF   **Register:** VIOLIN or ORGAN   **Sustain:** OFF

Play LH & RH hands separately at first, then together.

Moderately fast

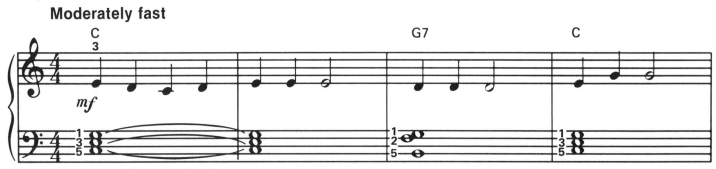

(TIED NOTES!)

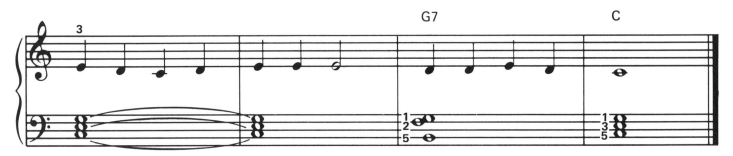

LARGO *(from "THE NEW WORLD")*

This melody is also known as *GOING HOME.* The word *"LARGO"* means "very slow."

Auto: OFF   **Rhythm:** OFF   **Register:** ORGAN, TRUMPET or HORN   **Sustain:** OFF

Play LH & RH hands separately at first, then together.

Dvorak

Slow

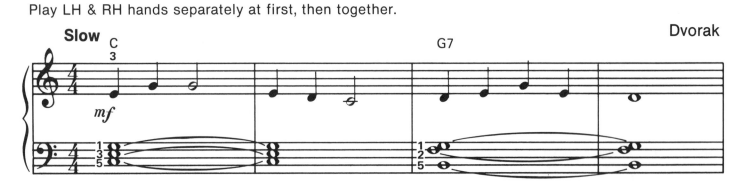

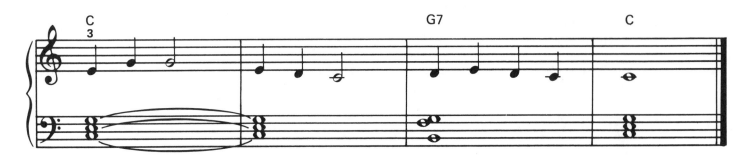

How to Play "Single Finger" 7th Chords

The "Single Finger" 7th chord actually requires 2 or more fingers to play, depending on the make of instrument you use.

On almost all makes other than YAMAHA, the 7th chord is made by playing THREE KEYS:

Play the KEY NOTE plus any TWO KEYS to the RIGHT, black or white. It is easiest to simply add the next TWO WHITE KEYS to the RIGHT.

For G7, play G, A & B. Use LH 3 2 1, or 4 3 2.

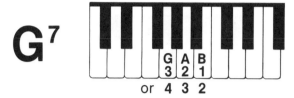

On YAMAHA instruments, the 7th chord is made by playing TWO KEYS:

Play the KEY NOTE plus any WHITE KEY to the LEFT. It is easiest to simply add the next WHITE KEY to the LEFT.

For G7, play F & G. Use LH 3 2.

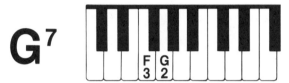

> IMPORTANT! On a few makes of instruments the 7th chord is formed in other ways.
> PLEASE CONSULT YOUR OWNER'S MANUAL.

HERE'S A HAPPY SONG! with RIGHT HAND Melody

Auto: ON "Single Finger"
Rhythm: Moderately fast SWING

Register: PIANO, MUSIC BOX or GUITAR
Sustain: ON

1. Play RH alone without Rhythm. (Do not press START or SYNCHRO/START.)
2. Add Rhythm: Press START. Adjust TEMPO. Count "1-2-3-4" for a few measures, then play RH again.
3. Add LH: Press SYNCHRO/START, then begin.
4. Add special effects, such as DUET and VARIATION, if you have them.
5. Play with ROCK 'N' ROLL rhythm, keeping the same tempo setting. Press START and listen to a few measures of rhythm alone, counting "1-2-3-4" at the same speed as for SWING rhythm. Press SYNCHRO/START, then play.

OPTIONAL: Play *MERRILY WE ROLL ALONG* (page 24) with Auto ON, using the same settings as for *HERE'S A HAPPY SONG.* Use "Single Finger" C and G7 chords.

Introducing (B) for Right Hand

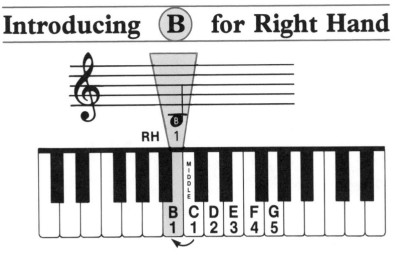

TO FIND B:

Place the RH in **C POSITION.**
Reach finger 1 one white key to the left!

Play slowly. Say the note names as you play.

Auto: OFF	**Register:** PIANO
Rhythm: OFF	**Sustain:** ON

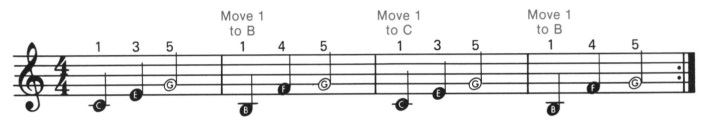

C & G⁷ Chords for Right Hand

It is very important to be able to play all chords with the RIGHT hand as well as the LEFT.
Chords are used in either or both hands in popular and classical music.

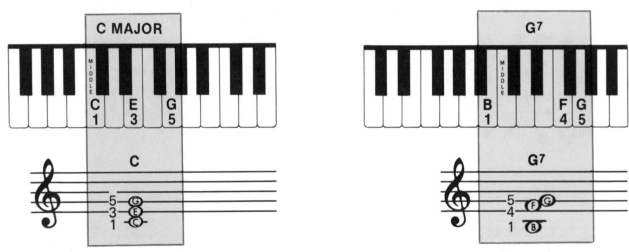

Practice changing from the C chord to the G⁷ chord and back again!

1. The 5th finger plays G in both chords.
2. The 4th finger plays F in the G⁷ chord.
3. Only the 1st finger moves out of C POSITION (down to B) for G⁷.

Auto: OFF   **Rhythm:** OFF   **Register:** PIANO   **Sustain:** ON

MARY ANN **with LH Melody**

Auto: OFF　　　　　　　　　　　　**Register:** PIANO, MUSIC BOX or VIBES
Rhythm: Moderately fast SWING　　**Sustain:** ON

1. Play without Auto Rhythm. (Do not touch START or SYNCHRO/START.)
2. Add Rhythm. Listen to a few measures of Rhythm. Count to adjust tempo. STOP the Rhythm.
   Press SYNCHRO/START, then begin.
3. Play again with ROCK 'N' ROLL rhythm at the same tempo.

Calypso tune

Moderately fast

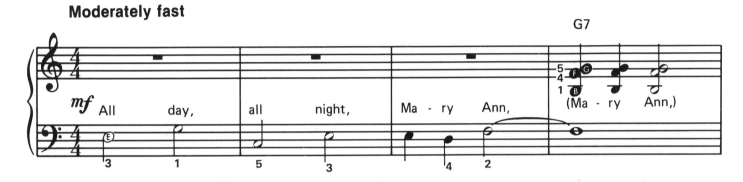

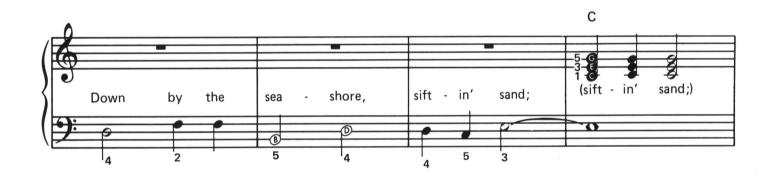

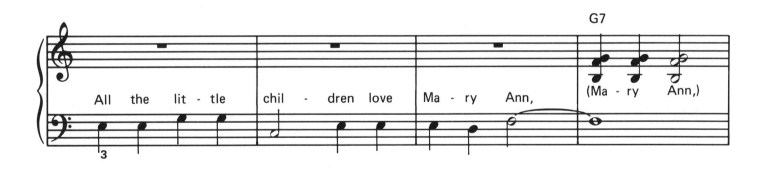

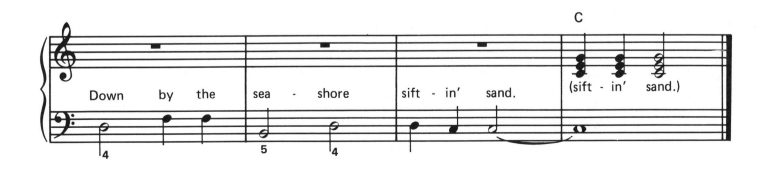

MARY ANN with RH Melody and Auto Chords

Auto: ON "Single Finger"
Rhythm: Moderately fast SWING or ROCK 'N' ROLL

Register: TRUMPET with Sustain OFF or
PIANO with Sustain ON

1. Press START/STOP, listen to Rhythm. Count to adjust tempo. STOP Rhythm.
2. Press SYNCHRO/START, then play hands together.
3. Play again. Add any other effects you wish, such as DUET, VARIATION, ARPEGGIO, VIBRATO, STEREO, REVERB, etc.*

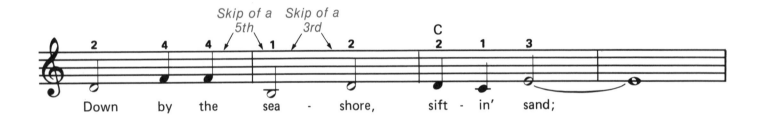

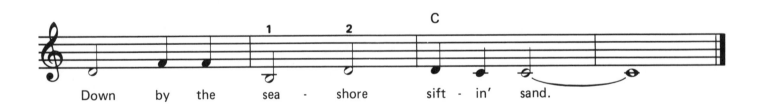

*VIBRATO produces a fluctuation in the sound, similar to the natural vibrato of the voice, or that produced on a violin or guitar by an oscillation of the finger holding the string down.

STEREO causes the sound to be distributed between the right and left speakers to produce a stereophonic effect, providing RH an orchestra-like presence.

REVERB produces a slight echo effect, simulating the sound of an instrument played in a concert hall.

These features are not available on all instruments.

New Time Signature

Dotted Half Note

3 means **3** beats to each measure.

4 means a **QUARTER NOTE** ♩ gets one beat.

A **DOTTED HALF NOTE** gets 3 counts.
(2 counts for the half note,
plus 1 count for the dot!)

COUNT: "1 - 2 - 3"

Clap (or tap) the following rhythm.

Clap **ONCE** for each note, counting aloud.

COUNT: 1 2 3 1 2 3 1 2 3 1 2 3

Set Auto Rhythm on WALTZ. Select a moderate, comfortable TEMPO. Press START and let the instrument beat a few measures. Clap or tap the above measures several times, counting "1-2-3" for each measure.

IMPORTANT! Always use WALTZ rhythm for music in ¾ time!

AN OLD-FASHIONED WALTZ

Auto: ON "Single Finger" **Register:** PIANO, HARPSICHORD or MUSIC BOX
Rhythm: WALTZ **Sustain:** ON

1. Use the same moderate tempo you used above. Press SYNCHRO/START, then play.
2. Play again, adding any effects you choose, such as DUET, VARIATION, ARPEGGIO, VIBRATO, etc.

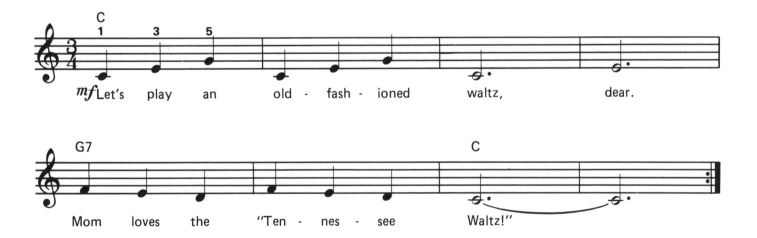

mf Let's play an old - fash - ioned waltz, dear.

Mom loves the "Ten - nes - see Waltz!"

NOTE: You can make the melody stand out more clearly by turning the *Chord* volume and *Rhythm* volume DOWN, and turning the *Master* volume UP!

Slurs & Legato Playing

A **SLUR** is a curved line over or under notes on *different* lines or spaces.

SLURS mean play **LEGATO** (smoothly connected).

Slurs often divide the music
into PHRASES.

A PHRASE is a musical thought
or sentence.

DON'T BUY ME RIBBONS

Auto: ON "Single Finger"
Rhythm: Moderately slow WALTZ

Register: PIANO, VIBES, MUSIC BOX, or GUITAR
Sustain: ON

1. Play RH alone without Rhythm. (Do not touch START or SYNCHRO/START.)
2. Add Rhythm: Press START. Listen, adjust tempo, then play RH.
3. Add LH: Press SYNCHRO/START and begin.
4. Add any extra effects you choose.

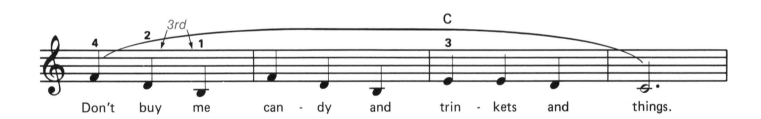

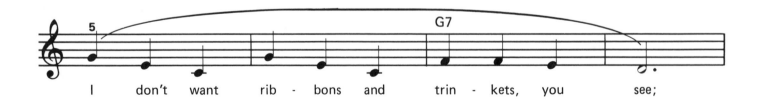

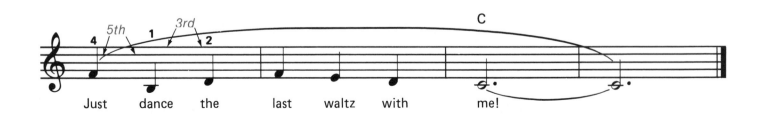

THE PEANUT SONG

Auto: ON "Single Finger" **Register:** ORGAN or TRUMPET
Rhythm: Moderately fast SWING **Sustain:** OFF

1. Play RH alone without Rhythm. (Do not touch START or SYNCHRO/START.)
2. Add Rhythm: Press START. Listen, adjust tempo, then play RH.
3. Add LH: Press SYNCHRO/START and begin.
4. Add any other effects you choose. Try different Registers, including PIANO and GUITAR with Sustain ON. Try other Rhythms, including SLOW ROCK, SHUFFLE and POP, if they are available.

NOTE: If the chords sound too soft during the FADE, you can remedy this by beginning the piece with the Auto volume turned up a little louder.

Introducing (A) for Left Hand

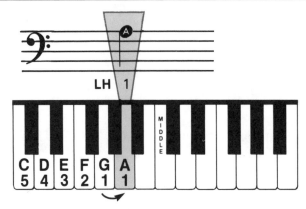

TO FIND A:

Place the LH in **C POSITION.**
Reach finger 1 one white key to the right!

Play slowly. Say the note names as you play.

Auto: OFF   **Register:** PIANO
Rhythm: OFF   **Sustain:** ON

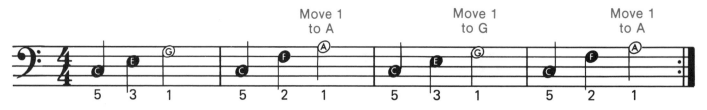

Introducing the F Major Chord

The C MAJOR chord is frequently followed by the F MAJOR chord, and vice-versa.

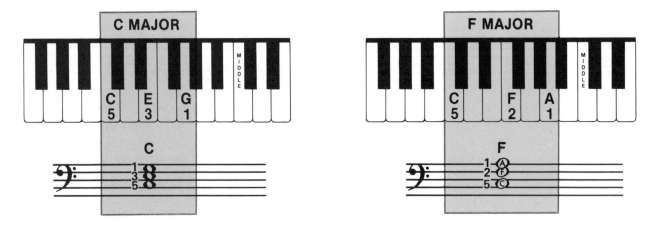

Practice changing from the C chord to the F chord and back again.

1. The 5th finger plays C in both chords.
2. The 2nd finger plays F in the F chord.
3. Only the 1st finger moves out of C POSITION (up to A) for the F chord.

Auto: OFF   **Rhythm:** OFF   **Register:** PIANO   **Sustain:** ON

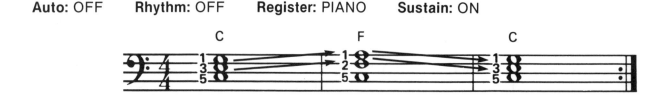

Warm-Up using C, G⁷ & F Chords

Practice SLOWLY at first, then gradually increase speed.

Auto: OFF   **Register:** TRUMPET
Rhythm: OFF   **Sustain:** OFF

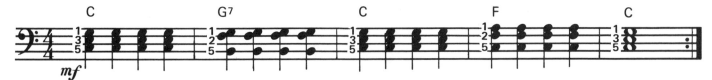

> **INCOMPLETE MEASURE:**
> Some pieces begin with an INCOMPLETE MEASURE. The 1st measure of this piece has only 3 counts. The missing count is found in the last measure! When you repeat the whole song, you will have one whole measure of 4 counts when you play the last measure plus the first measure.

WHEN THE SAINTS GO MARCHING IN

Auto: OFF   **Register:** TRUMPET
Rhythm: OFF   **Sustain:** OFF

The Single Finger F Major Chord

REMINDER: When Auto is ON, you can make the Single Finger F MAJOR CHORD by playing only ONE key. Play the lowest F key on your instrument with LH 2.

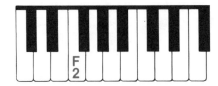

WHEN THE SAINTS GO MARCHING IN
with Automatic Chords & Rhythm

You will enjoy playing this piece with Auto Rhythm.
Select a march-like rhythm. If you select MARCH, use a rather SLOW tempo at first.
(On some instruments, MARCH rhythm beats in double time!)

Auto: ON "Single Finger" **Register:** TRUMPET, CLARINET, SAX or TROMBONE
Rhythm: MARCH, SWING or POP **Sustain:** OFF

1. Start the Rhythm and count "1-2-3-4" for a few measures to adjust the tempo to a comfortable speed. Stop the Rhythm.
2. Play with hands together. Press SYNCHRO/START. Play the RH "pick-up" notes, then play the 1st LH key exactly on the note above which the symbol C appears.

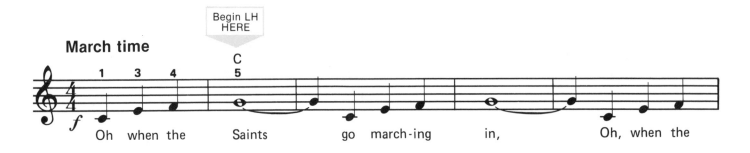

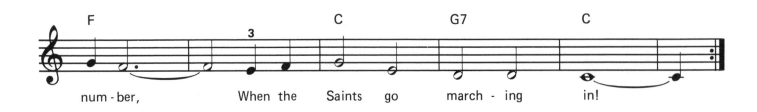

3. Play again. Add any other effects you choose, such as DUET, VARIATION, ARPEGGIOS, VIBRATO, STEREO, etc.

ROCK ANYWHERE!

Auto: ON "Single Finger"
Rhythm: Moderately fast SWING or slow ROCK 'N' ROLL

Register: GUITAR or PIANO with Sustain ON, or TRUMPET or SYNTHE with Sustain OFF

1. Start Rhythm. Count a few measures, adjust tempo. Play RH alone.
2. Add LH: Press SYNCHRO/START and begin. Listen to what the Auto Rhythm plays during the whole rests.

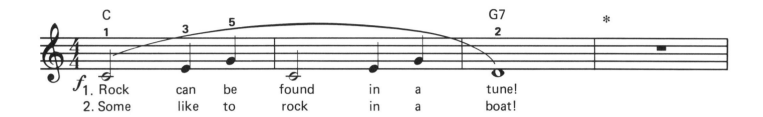

1. Rock can be found in a tune!
2. Some like to rock in a boat!

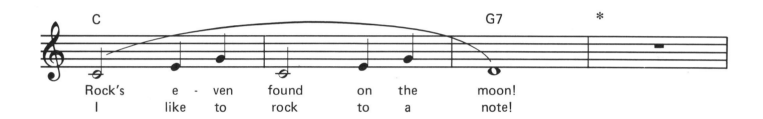

Rock's e - ven found on the moon!
I like to rock to a note!

Grand - fa - ther rocks in his old rock - in' chair, So I
Mom used to rock me to sleep with a song, So I've

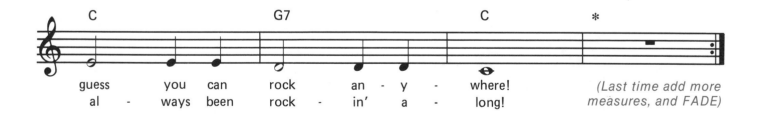

guess you can rock an - y - where!
al - ways been rock - in' a - long!

(Last time add more measures, and FADE)

★Adding "Fill Ins"

Many instruments have a button at the left of the keyboard or a bar on the left edge of the keyboard, marked "FILL IN." This feature causes the Rhythm to play a fancy drum break when the button or bar is pressed. This effect is best used during a long rest, or when the melody is held for one or more entire measures. For example, you can use it by pressing the FILL IN button or bar on the first count of each whole rest in *ROCK ANYWHERE.* See the asterisks (∗) above. The FILL IN effect is always OPTIONAL.

Introducing (A) for Right Hand

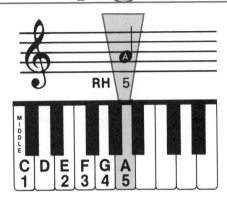

TO FIND A:

Place the RH in **C POSITION.**
Leave 1 on C.
Shift all other fingers one white key to the right!

Play slowly. Say the note names as you play.

Auto: OFF   **Register:** PIANO
Rhythm: OFF   **Sustain:** ON

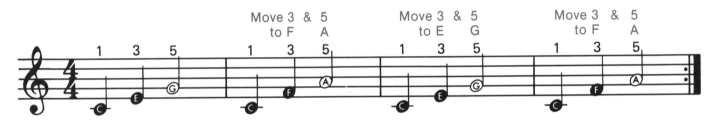

C & F Chords for Right Hand

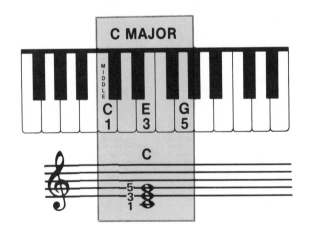

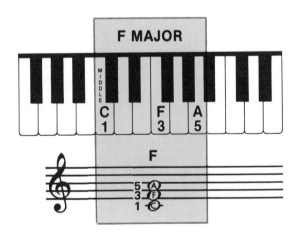

Practice changing from the C chord to the F chord and back again:
1.   The 1st finger plays C in both chords.
2.   The 3rd finger moves up to F and the 5th finger moves up to A for the F chord.

Auto: OFF   **Rhythm:** OFF   **Register:** PIANO   **Sustain:** ON

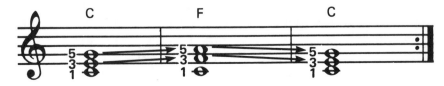

OLD COUNTRY MUSIC

Auto: ON "Single Finger"
Rhythm: Moderately fast SWING, COUNTRY or SLOW ROCK

Register: GUITAR or PIANO with Sustain ON, or TRUMPET or SYNTHE with Sustain OFF

1. Play RH alone without Auto Rhythm.
2. Add Rhythm: Count a few measures, adjust tempo. Play RH alone. Stop Rhythm.
3. Add LH: Press SYNCHRO and begin.
4. Add DUET, VARIATION, STEREO and/or other effects.

TRY A *FADE ENDING!* Just take your hands OFF the keys, and let the Rhythm continue playing automatically. Gradually turn the Master volume control down until the music fades completely away.

*OPTIONAL: Add FILL IN.

G Position

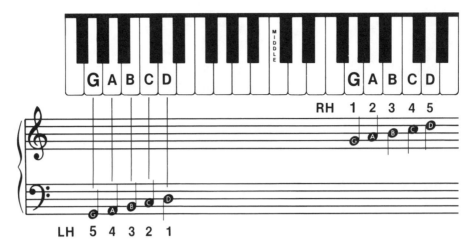

Auto: OFF   **Rhythm:** OFF   **Register:** PIANO   **Sustain:** ON

Play and say the note names. Be sure to do this SEVERAL TIMES!

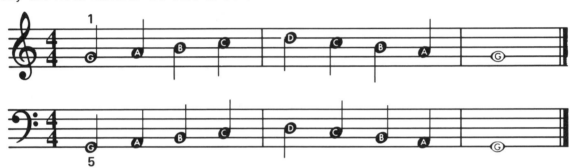

Intervals in G Position

1. MELODIC INTERVALS

Say the name of each interval as you play.

Auto: OFF   **Register:** PIANO
Rhythm: OFF   **Sustain:** ON

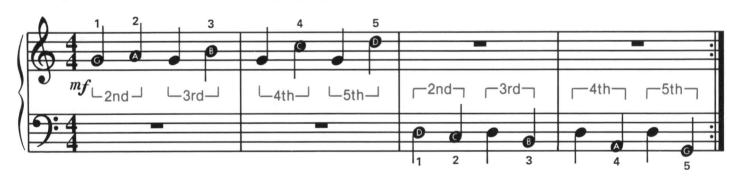

2. HARMONIC INTERVALS

Say the name of each interval as you play.

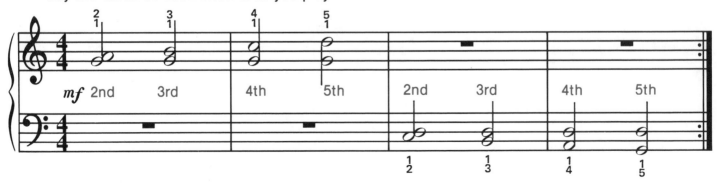

LOVE SOMEBODY!

G POSITION

Auto: OFF **Register:** ELECTRIC PIANO or MUSIC BOX
Rhythm: OFF **Sustain:** ON

Before playing hands together, play LH alone, naming each harmonic interval!

Happily

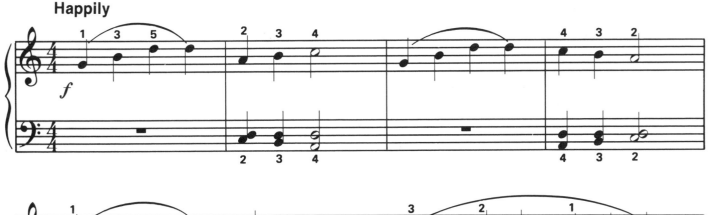

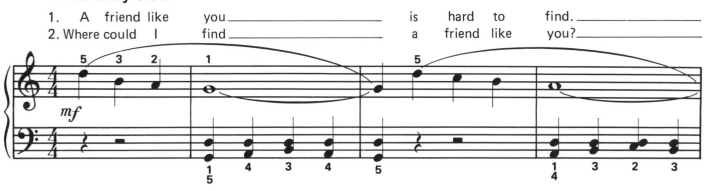

A FRIEND LIKE YOU

G POSITION

Auto: OFF **Register:** TRUMPET or ORGAN
Rhythm: OFF **Sustain:** OFF

Before playing hands together, play LH alone, naming each harmonic interval!

Moderately slow

1. A friend like you_____ is hard to find._____
2. Where could I find_____ a friend like you?_____

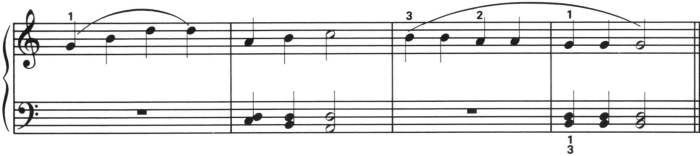

_____ You're al-ways true,_____ You're al-ways kind._____
_____ A friend so kind,_____ so good, so true._____

You can play *LOVE SOMEBODY* and *A FRIEND LIKE YOU* with moderately fast SWING RHYTHM.
Press SYNCHRO/START and begin. Rhythm will begin when the LH plays its first pair of notes.

The Sharp Sign

The **SHARP SIGN** before a note means play the next key to the RIGHT, whether black or white!

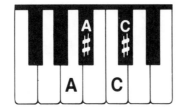

When a SHARP (♯) appears before a note, it applies to that note for the rest of the measure!

Circle the notes that are SHARP:

MONEY CAN'T BUY EV'RYTHING!

Auto: OFF
Rhythm: Moderately fast SWING or ROCK

Register: BANJO, PIANO or GUITAR
Sustain: ON

1. Play RH alone without Rhythm.
2. Add Rhythm: Check tempo, then play. Stop Rhythm.
3. Add LH: Press SYNCHRO and begin. Rhythm will begin when LH plays.

G POSITION

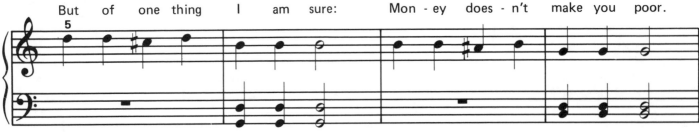

MONEY CAN'T BUY EV'RYTHING!
with Single Finger Chords

> This sign is called a **FERMATA**.
>
> Hold the note under the FERMATA longer than its value.

A two-measure *introduction** and a three-measure *ending** have been added to this version. From the *introduction* you can get the feel of the tempo and rhythm by the time the RH melody begins to play. The *fermata,* mentioned above, will be used in the *ending.*

> **THE D7 CHORD:** You will be using the D7 chord for the first time.
> - On most instruments this is played by adding two keys above the **D.**
>   **Play three white keys, D E & F, with 3 2 1 or 4 3 2.**
> - On **YAMAHA** instruments add **one white key BELOW the D. Play C & D with 3 2.**

Auto: ON "Single Finger"   **Register:** BANJO, PIANO or GUITAR
Rhythm: Moderately fast SWING   **Sustain:** ON

1. Press SYNCHRO and play LH alone. Adjust tempo and begin again, if necessary. In the very last measure play LH G again and HOLD IT. At the same time, press the STOP button with the RH. Let the sound of the final chord continue as long as you wish.
2. Play with BOTH hands. Press SYNCHRO and begin with LH. Add RH after counting "1-2-3-4" twice for the two measure intro.
3. Play again, adding VARIATION & DUET, if available.

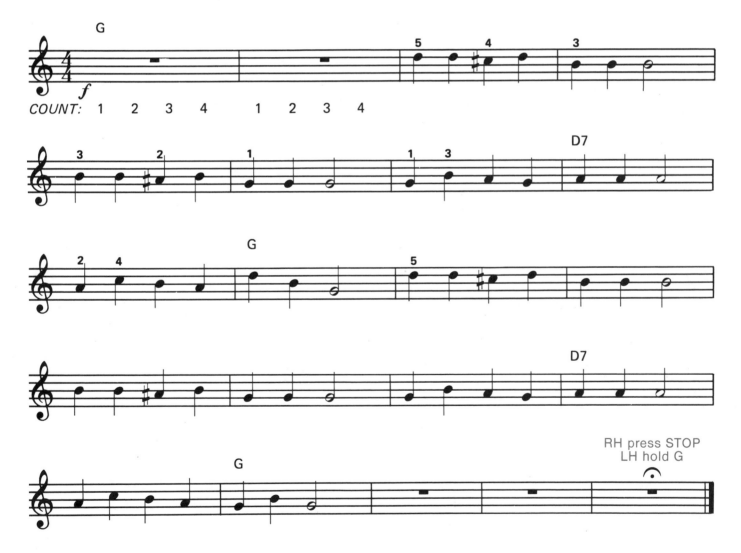

*If your instrument has *intro* and *ending* buttons, you may wish to use them here.
Please check your OWNER'S MANUAL.

The G Major & D⁷ Chords for Left Hand

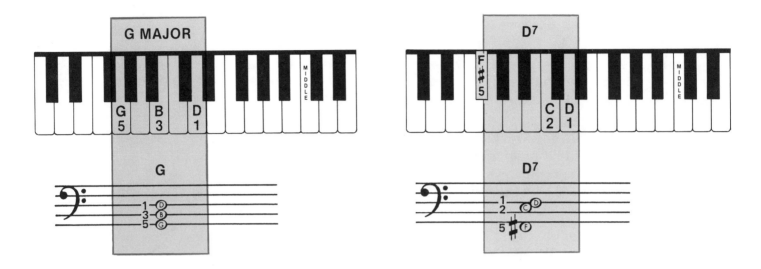

Practice changing from the G chord to the D⁷ and back again:

1. 1 Plays D in both chords.
2. 2 plays C in the D⁷ chord.
3. Only 5 moves out of G POSITION (down to F♯) for D⁷.

Auto: OFF   **Rhythm:** OFF   **Register:** PIANO   **Sustain:** ON

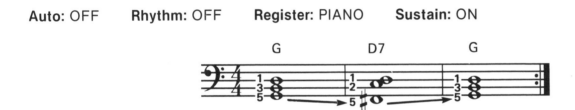

Play the following several times. Use the same keyboard settings as shown above.

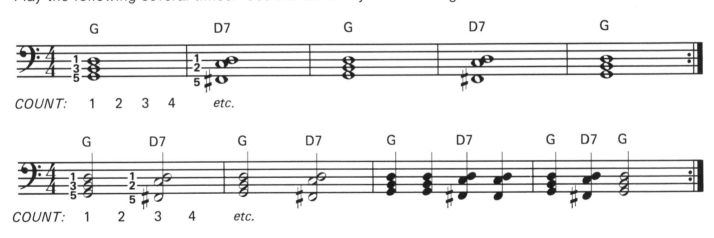

Preparation for *THE CUCKOO.*

COUNT: 1   2   3   *etc.*

THE CUCKOO

Auto: OFF   **Register:** PIANO, ELECTRONIC PIANO or MUSIC BOX
Rhythm: OFF   **Sustain:** ON

Play hands separately, then together, counting aloud.

Moderately slow to moderately fast   Folk song

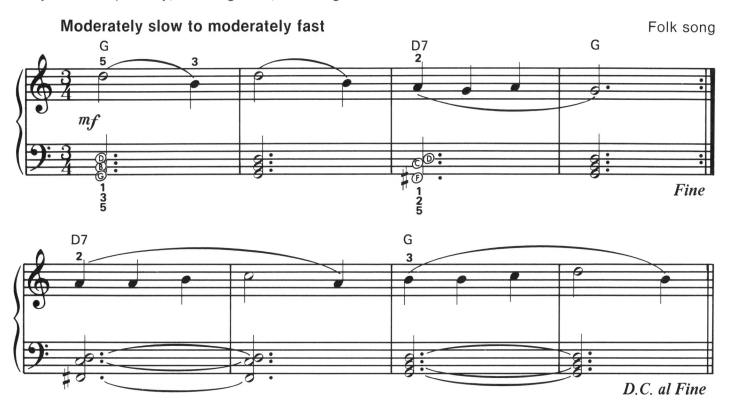

D.C. al Fine (Da Capo al Fine) means repeat from the beginning and play to the end *(Fine)*.

Fingered Chords

The "Fingered Chord" feature of your instrument can be used when you form your own chords and all the notes are within the range of the accompaniment section of your instrument. Among the advantages of this feature are the following:

- You can control the volume of the chord separately from the volume of the melody, and thus bring the melody out louder than the chords.
- You can form any chord, including those that are not possible with the "Single Finger" feature.
- All of the automatic features of the "Single Finger" setting, such as VARIATION, DUET, ARPEGGIO, and the various RHYTHMS, may be used with "Fingered Chord." They will sound the same.
- You will be getting practice in forming your own chords, and you can use this knowledge to play a keyboard instrument that does not have a "Single Finger" feature, such as a piano, organ, or synthesizer.

1. Play *THE CUCKOO* again, exactly as before, with Auto ON "Fingered Chord" setting.
   Do not use Rhythm.

2. Play *THE CUCKOO* again, with the following setting:
   Auto: ON "Fingered Chord"   **Register:** PIANO, ELECTRONIC PIANO or MUSIC BOX
   Rhythm: Moderately slow WALTZ   **Sustain:** ON

   Press SYNCHRO and play. You can release each chord after you play it. The sounds will continue until you play the next chord, just as when "Single Finger" is used.

3. Add DUET, VARIATION, ARPEGGIO and/or any other effects you choose.

OPTIONAL: Let the Rhythm continue for a few measures after the *Fine,* and FADE.

The G Major & D⁷ Chords for Right Hand

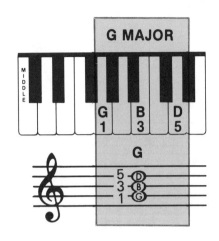
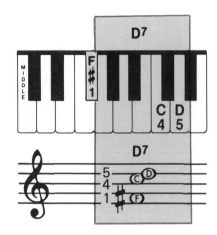

Practice changing from the G chord to the D⁷ chord and back again:

1. 5 plays D in both chords.
2. 4 plays C in the D⁷ chord.
3. Only 1 moves out of G POSITION (down to F♯) for D⁷.

Auto: OFF   **Rhythm:** OFF   **Register:** PIANO   **Sustain:** ON

Play several times. Use the same keyboard settings as shown above.

G Major & D⁷ Chords, Block & Broken

REMINDER: When all three notes of a chord are played together, it is a BLOCK CHORD.
When the notes of a chord are played separately, it is a BROKEN CHORD.

Play several times. Use the same keyboard settings as shown above.

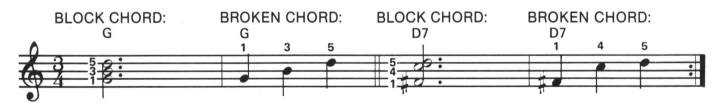

Play with LH. **Auto:** OFF   **Register:** PIANO   **Sustain:** ON

The Sustaining Pedal

A SUSTAINING PEDAL is available for many electronic keyboards. It plugs into the back of the instrument. When you hold the pedal down it causes the tones to sustain longer.

You must release the pedal between notes made on such Registers as ORGAN, TRUMPET or VIOLIN, or the tones will overlap.

Use the RIGHT FOOT to press the pedal. Keep the heel on the floor. Use your ankle like a hinge.

This sign means: PEDAL DOWN   PEDAL UP

└─────────────────── HOLD PEDAL ───────────────────┘

If you do not have a sustaining pedal, ignore the pedal signs.

STUDY IN G MAJOR

1. Play first with the following setting: **Auto:** ON "Fingered Chord"   **Rhythm:** OFF
   Register: Try several different ones with Sustain OFF if you have a sustaining pedal. Otherwise use Sustain ON.

2. Play again with moderately slow WALTZ rhythm. You do not have to hold each chord. You will hear the chords only on the 2nd and 3rd counts of the rhythmic beats.

3. Add ARPEGGIOS or VARIATION, stereo, vibrato and/or other effects.

Moderately slow

A New Position of the C Major Chord

You have already played the C MAJOR CHORD with C as the lowest note: that is **C E G.**
When you play these same 3 notes in any order, you still have a C MAJOR CHORD.
When you are playing in G POSITION, it is most convenient to play G as the lowest note: **G C E.**

The following diagrams show how easy it is to move from the G MAJOR CHORD to the
C MAJOR CHORD, when G is the lowest note of both chords.

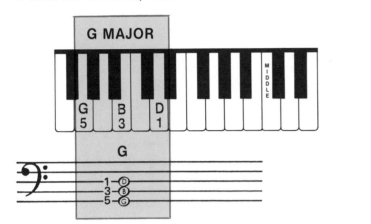 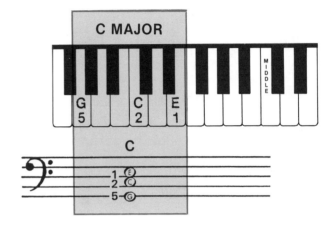

Practice changing from the G chord to the C chord and back again:
1. 5 plays G in both chords.
2. 2 plays C in the C chord.
3. Only 1 moves out of G POSITION (up to E) for the C chord.

Auto: ON "Fingered Chord"
Rhythm: OFF

Preparation for Beautiful Brown Eyes

1. Play the following with **Auto:** ON "Fingered Chord"   **Rhythm:** OFF   **Register:** GUITAR or PIANO.
2. Play again with **Auto:** ON "Fingered Chord"   **Rhythm:** Moderately slow WALTZ.
    Press SYNCHRO, then begin. You need not hold each chord. The chords will sound on the 2nd
    and 3rd counts of each measure.
3. Play again, adding VARIATION or ARPEGGIO effects.

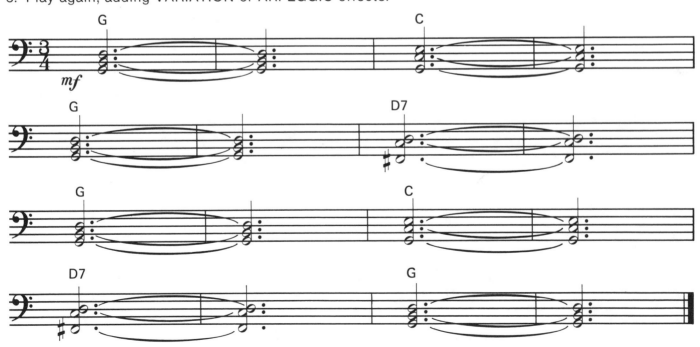

BEAUTIFUL BROWN EYES

Auto: ON "Fingered Chord"
Rhythm: Moderately fast WALTZ

Register: GUITAR or PIANO
Sustain: ON (if you have no sustaining pedal).
If you have a sustaining pedal, use any register you wish.

1. Play RH alone.
2. Add LH: Press SYNCHRO, then begin. You do not have to hold the chords. You will hear the chords only in the rhythmic beats.
3. Play again, adding VARIATION or ARPEGGIO, and other effects.

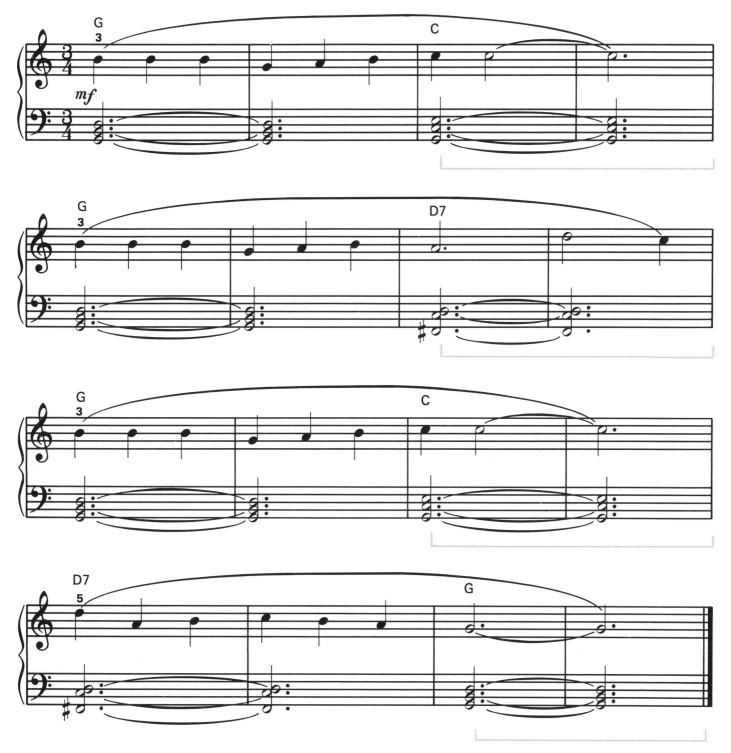

4. Play *BEAUTIFUL BROWN EYES* again, using the same Rhythm and Register, but with Auto ON "Single Finger Chord." Use the "single finger" method of playing the G major chord, etc. The sound is really no different than when "Fingered Chord" is used. Only the manner of playing is different!

Introducing E for Right Hand

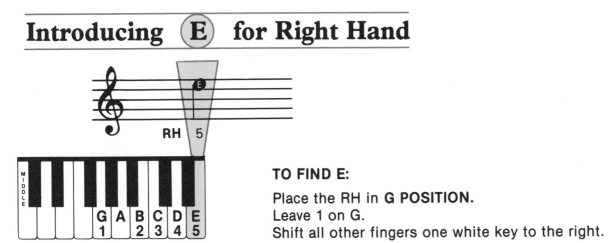

TO FIND E:

Place the RH in **G POSITION.**
Leave 1 on G.
Shift all other fingers one white key to the right.

Play slowly. Say the note names as you play.

Auto: OFF	**Register:** PIANO
Rhythm: OFF	**Sustain:** ON

New C Major Chord Position—Right Hand

Notice that TWO fingers must move to the right when changing from the G MAJOR CHORD to the C MAJOR CHORD.

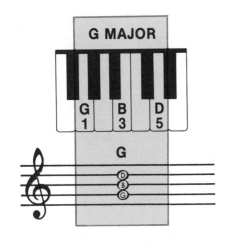

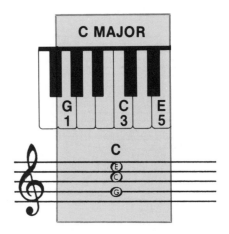

Practice changing from the G chord to the C chord and back again:

1. 1 plays G in both chords.
2. 3 moves up to C and 5 moves up to E for the C chord.

Auto: OFF   **Rhythm:** OFF   **Register:** PIANO   **Sustain:** ON

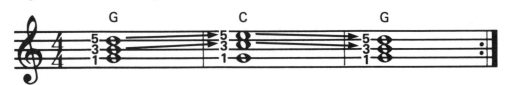

ALPINE MELODY

The RH of this piece combines BLOCK CHORDS and BROKEN CHORDS, which are the same as the BLOCK CHORDS played in the LH in each measure!

1. Use the following setting:

   Auto: ON "Fingered Chord"   **Rhythm:** OFF   **Register:** PIANO or ORGAN

   Sustain: OFF (if you have no sustaining pedals, use Sustain: ON).

   Play the hands separately, then together.

2. Add Rhythm: Moderately slow WALTZ. Press SYNCHRO and play hands together.
   You need not hold the LH chords. The rhythm that continues to sound after each chord is released contains the chord you played.

3. Play again, adding VARIATION or ARPEGGIO and other effects. Do not use DUET.

Moderately slow

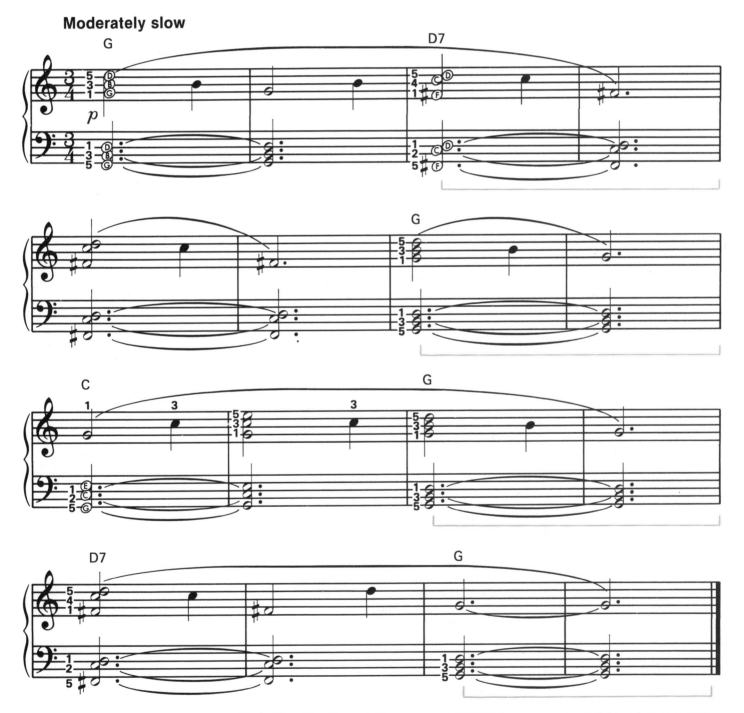

Stop the Rhythm at the end, or FADE for several additional measures.

4. Play *ALPINE MELODY* again, using the same Rhythm and Register, but with Auto ON "Single Finger Chord." Use the "single finger" method of playing the G major chord, etc.

   IMPORTANT: Repeat with a different Register, such as MUSIC BOX or VIBES.

Eighth Notes

Two eighth notes are played in the time of **one quarter note.**

When a piece contains eighth notes,
count: "**1 · &**" for each quarter note;
count: "**1 · &**" for each pair of eighth notes.

Clap (or tap) these notes, counting aloud.

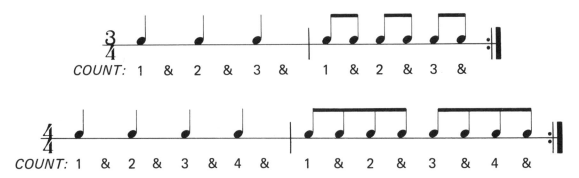

Play these few measures of *GOOD MORNING TO YOU* and *HAPPY BIRTHDAY TO YOU**.
These measures show, in a simple way, the difference between quarter notes and eighth notes.
Use any Register. Play without Rhythm. All the examples on this page are in C POSITION.

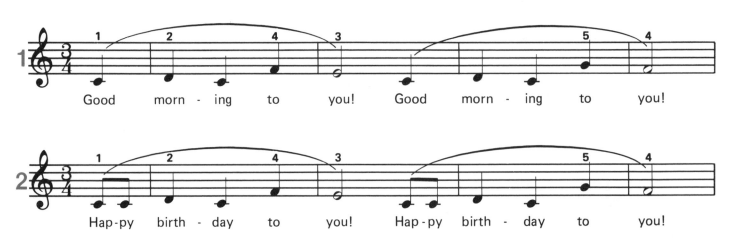

Play these two examples with eighth notes used in $\frac{4}{4}$ time. Use any Register.

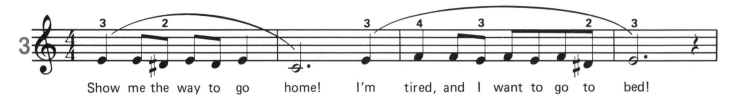

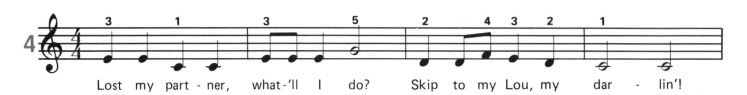

SKIP TO MY LOU

Auto: ON "Single Finger" **Register:** ORGAN, TRUMPET or SYNTHE
Rhythm: Very slow MARCH or Moderately fast SWING **Sustain:** ON

1. Play RH alone without Rhythm, counting aloud.
2. Add Rhythm: Press START, listen to a few measures, adjust tempo and play RH.
3. Add LH, using the "single finger" method of playing chords. Press SYNCHRO and begin.
4. Add VARIATION or ARPEGGIO effects, plus DUET, STEREO, VIBRATO, etc.

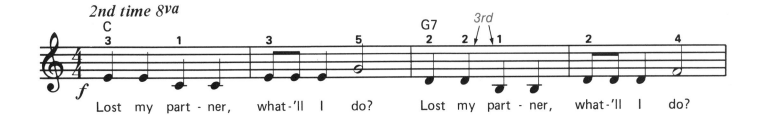

CHORUS

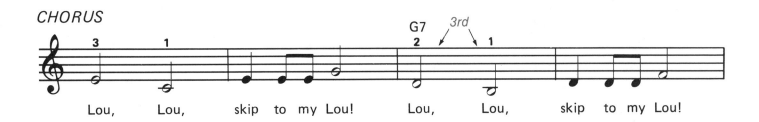

Notes played between the main beats of the measure
and held across the beat are called **SYNCOPATED NOTES.**

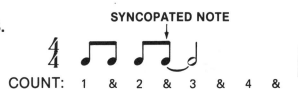

SYNCOPATED NOTE

COUNT: 1 & 2 & 3 & 4 &

STANDING IN THE NEED OF PRAYER

This piece, in G POSITION, may be played with "Fingered Chord" or "Single Finger" setting.
It is beneficial to learn to play it BOTH ways!

Rhythm: Very slow MARCH or Moderately fast SWING
Register: ORGAN with Sustain OFF or PIANO with Sustain ON

1. Play RH alone without Rhythm. Count aloud.
2. Add Rhythm: Press START and play.
3. Add LH: Press SYNCHRO and begin.

Introducing Dotted Quarter Notes

A DOT INCREASES THE LENGTH OF A NOTE BY ONE HALF ITS VALUE.

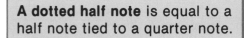

A dotted half note is equal to a half note tied to a quarter note.

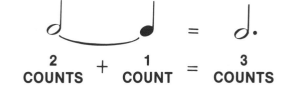

| 2 COUNTS | + | 1 COUNT | = | 3 COUNTS |

A **dotted quarter note** is equal to a quarter note tied to an eighth note.

The single eighth note is written like this:

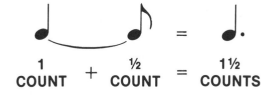

| 1 COUNT | + | ½ COUNT | = | 1½ COUNTS |

Clap (or tap) the following rhythm. Clap **ONCE** for each note, counting aloud.

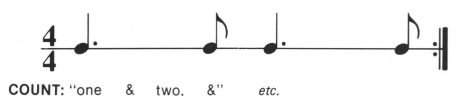

COUNT: "one & two, &" *etc.*

The only difference in the following two measures and those directly above them is the way they are written. They are played the same.

COUNT: "one & two, &" *etc.*

In $\frac{4}{4}$ or $\frac{3}{4}$ time, the DOTTED QUARTER NOTE is almost ALWAYS followed by an EIGHTH NOTE!

Here are two excerpts from familiar tunes using dotted quarter notes. Both examples are in C POSITION.

1. Count and clap (or tap) the notes.
2. Play and count. Use any Register you wish.
3. Play and sing the words.

Si - lent night, Ho - ly night,

Here comes the bride! All dressed in white!

KUM-BA-YAH!*

C POSITION

In this favorite song, you will be using the C major and F major chords in the RH.

Auto: ON "Single Finger" **Register:** PIANO or GUITAR
Rhythm: Very slow DISCO or very slow MARCH **Sustain:** ON

1. Play RH alone, counting aloud.
2. Add Rhythm.
3. Add LH: Press SYNCHRO and begin.

1. Kum - ba - yah, my Lord, Kum - ba - yah! Kum - ba -
2. Some - one's pray - ing, Lord, Kum - ba - yah! Some - one's

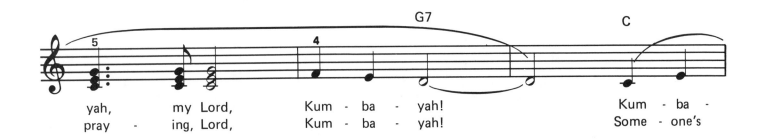

yah, my Lord, Kum - ba - yah! Kum - ba -
pray - ing, Lord, Kum - ba - yah! Some - one's

yah, my Lord, Kum - ba - yah! Oh
pray - ing, Lord, Kum - ba - yah! Oh

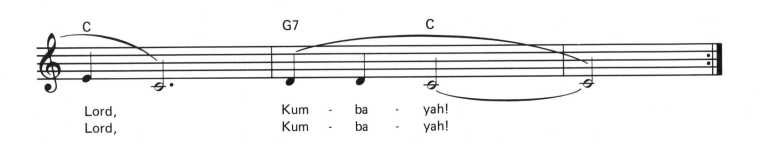

Lord, Kum - ba - yah!
Lord, Kum - ba - yah!

*Kum-ba-yah means "Come by here."

THINK ABOUT THE HAPPY DAYS!

G POSITION

This piece should be played with a DRIVING rhythm. It is not a slow, sad song!

Practice it with Auto ON "Single Finger" and with "Fingered Chord."

Rhythm: Moderately fast SLOW ROCK   **Register:** TRUMPET or SAX   **Sustain:** OFF

1. Play RH alone. Count.
2. Add Rhythm.
3. Add LH: Press SYNCHRO and begin.
4. Add DUET, if available. Do not add VARIATION or ARPEGGIO.

Measuring 6ths

When you skip 4 white keys, the interval is a **6th**.

6ths are written
line-space
or
space-line.

RH

This is C POSITION plus 1 note (A) played with 5.

RH 5 plays G or A!

Say the names of these intervals as you play!

Auto: OFF   **Register:** PIANO
Rhythm: OFF   **Sustain:** ON

MELODIC INTERVALS:

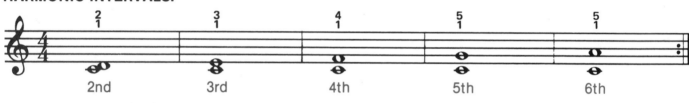

2nd   3rd   4th   5th   6th

HARMONIC INTERVALS:

2nd   3rd   4th   5th   6th

LH

This is C POSITION plus 1 note (A) played with 1!

LH 1 plays G or A!

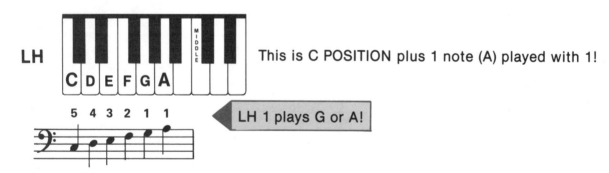

Say the names of these intervals as you play!

Auto: OFF   **Register:** PIANO
Rhythm: OFF   **Sustain:** ON

MELODIC INTERVALS:

2nd   3rd   4th   5th   6th

HARMONIC INTERVALS:

2nd   3rd   4th   5th   6th

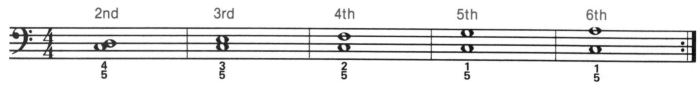

In *LAVENDER'S BLUE*, 5ths and 6ths are played with 1 & 5. Play this WARM-UP several times before playing *LAVENDER'S BLUE*. Use any Register.

LAVENDER'S BLUE

C POSITION + 1

Auto: ON "Single Finger"   **Rhythm:** Moderate WALTZ   **Register:** PIANO   **Sustain:** ON

1. Play RH alone.
2. Add Rhythm. Check tempo before playing, counting a few measures.
3. Add LH: Press SYNCHRO and begin. *Ritardando,* at the end, means "slowing down the tempo."
   As the LH chords continue to play, gradually move the TEMPO slide or knob to its slowest setting with the RH. On the *fermata,* in the last measure, hold the LH C and press STOP with the RH. The final LH chord will continue to sound as long as you hold the LH C.
4. Add VARIATION or ARPEGGIO, DUET and other effects.

ritardando (slowing down tempo)

58

London Bridge

When you play in positions that include 6 or more notes, any finger may be required to play 2 notes.

Auto: ON "Single Finger"
Rhythm: Moderately slow SLOW ROCK or SWING
Register: MUSIC BOX, PICCOLO or SYNTH FLUTE
Sustain: OFF

1. Play RH with Rhythm. Adjust tempo before beginning.
2. Add LH: Press SYNCHRO and begin.

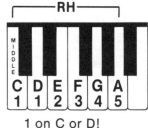

1 on C or D!

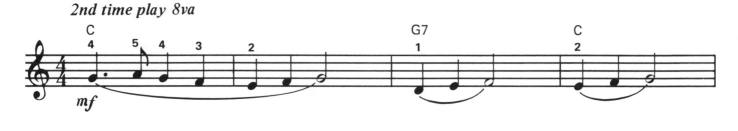

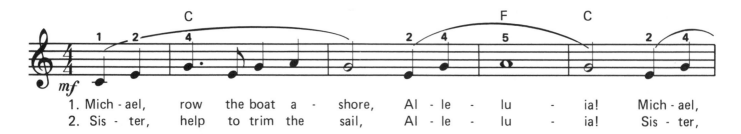

Michael, Row the Boat Ashore

Auto: ON "Single Finger"
Rhythm: Very slow MARCH or moderately slow SWING
Register: TRUMPET, SAX or ORGAN
Sustain: OFF

1. Play RH with Rhythm. Adjust tempo before beginning.
2. Add LH: Press SYNCHRO and begin.

POSITON for 1st LINE:
RH 1 PLAYS C, 2 PLAYS E

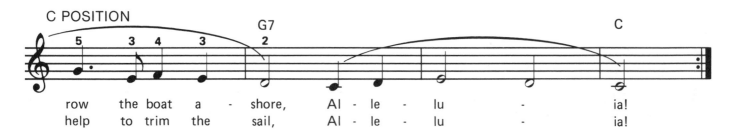

BLOW THE MAN DOWN!

Auto: ON "Single Finger"
Rhythm: Moderate WALTZ
Register: ORGAN, TRUMPET or OBOE
Sustain: OFF

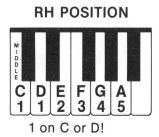

RH POSITION

1 on C or D!

1. Play RH with Rhythm. Adjust tempo before beginning.
2. Add LH: Press SYNCHRO and begin.
   Play LH C exactly with the RH note above which the C appears.
3. Add VARIATION, DUET, VIBRATO, or other effects. Experiment with various Registers, such as PIANO, SYNTHE, VIOLIN, etc.

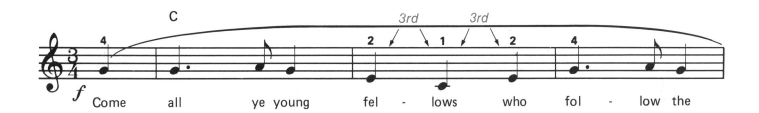

Come all ye young fel - lows who fol - low the

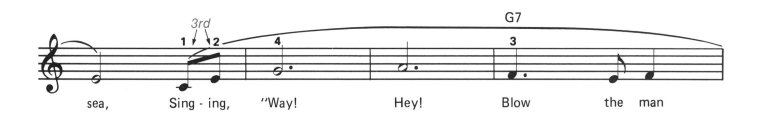

sea, Sing - ing, "Way! Hey! Blow the man

down!" And please pay at - ten - tion and lis - ten to

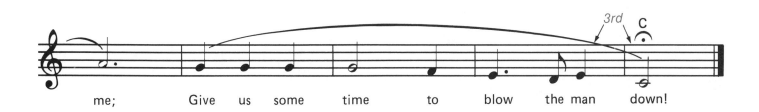

me; Give us some time to blow the man down!

At the end, you may HOLD the last LH C and press the STOP button with the RH either immediately after playing the RH C, or after the 2nd count of the final measure.

Moving Up & Down the Keyboard in 6ths

This exercise will prepare you to move freely up and down the keyboard. READ ONLY THE LOWEST NOTE OF EACH HARMONIC INTERVAL, adding a 6th above!

Begin with RH 1 on MIDDLE C.

LONE STAR WALTZ

Auto: ON "Single Finger" **Register:** PIANO, ELECTRONIC PIANO or MUSIC BOX
Rhythm: Moderately slow WALTZ **Sustain:** ON

1. Play RH with Rhythm. Adjust tempo before beginning.
2. Add LH: Press SYNCHRO and begin.
3. Add other effects.

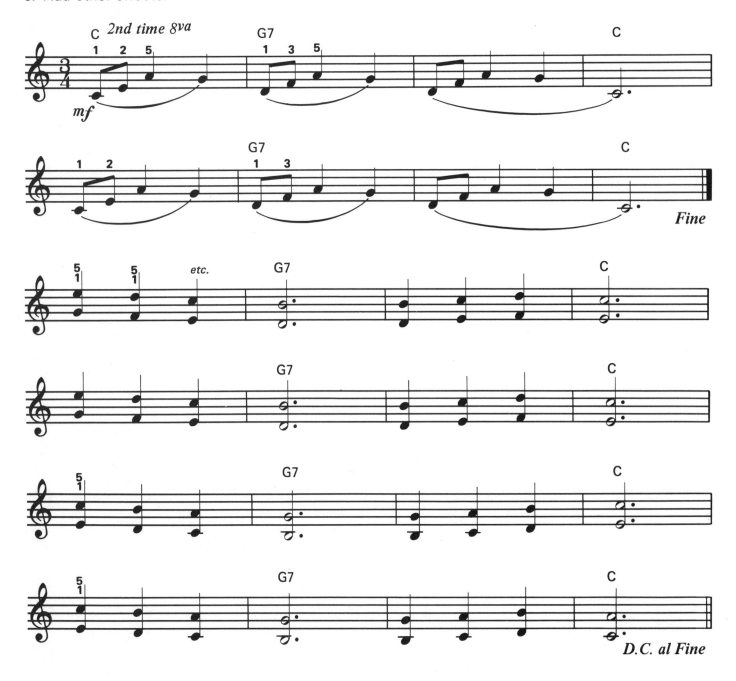

This is an EIGHTH REST: ♇
Rest for the value of
one eighth note ♪

Count and clap (or tap) the rhythm:

COUNT: 1 & 2 & 3 & 4 &

THE HOKEY-POKEY

Auto: ON "Single Finger"   **Register:** ORGAN
Rhythm: Moderately fast SWING or SLOW ROCK   **Sustain:** OFF

1. Play RH without Rhythm, counting aloud.
2. Add Rhythm: Press START, adjust tempo, then play along with RH.
3. Add LH: Press SYNCHRO and begin. Play first LH note at the beginning of the 2nd line.

2nd time
LH press STOP

Repeat from ‖:
(See end of 1st line)

Measuring 7ths & Octaves

When you skip 5 white keys,
the interval is a **7th**.

When you skip 6 white keys,
the interval is an **OCTAVE**.

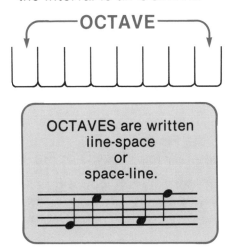

7ths are written
line-line
or
space-space.

OCTAVES are written
line-space
or
space-line.

Say the names of these intervals as you play!

Auto: OFF   **Register:** PIANO
Rhythm: OFF   **Sustain:** ON

RH MELODIC INTERVALS:

RH HARMONIC INTERVALS:

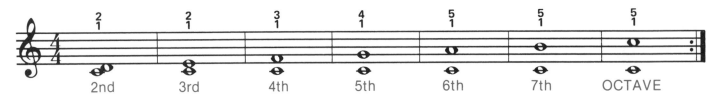

LH MELODIC INTERVALS:

LH HARMONIC INTERVALS:

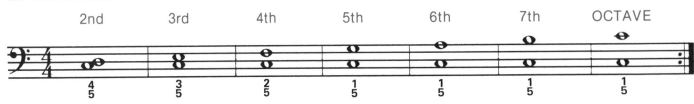

Café Vienna

Auto: ON "Single Finger"
Rhythm: Moderately fast WALTZ

Register: VIOLIN with Sustain OFF, or
PIANO or MUSIC BOX with Sustain ON

1. Play RH without Rhythm. Count aloud.
2. Add Rhythm.
3. Add LH: Press SYNCHRO and begin.
4. Add DUET, STEREO, ARPEGGIO, and other effects.

OPTIONAL: Hold the last RH note and FADE, using the LH to gradually turn the volume down.

The Flat Sign

The **FLAT SIGN** before a note means play the next key to the LEFT, whether black or white.

When a FLAT (♭) appears before a note, it applies to that note for the rest of the measure.

Circle the notes that are FLAT:

ROCK IT AWAY!

Auto: ON "Single Finger"
Rhythm: Moderately slow SWING or SLOW ROCK

Register: TRUMPET or SAX
Sustain: OFF   Add DUET, if available.

1. Play RH without Rhythm.
2. Add Rhythm.
3. Add LH.

2nd time 8va

If you're feel - in' blue,   if you're   feel - in' kind - a   wear - y,

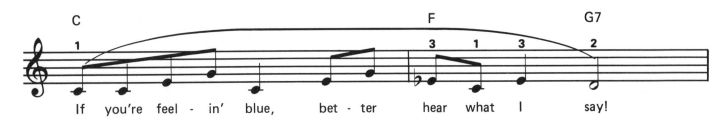

If you're feel - in' blue,   bet - ter   hear   what   I   say!

Play this rock - in' tune,   it will   sure - ly   make you   cheer - y;

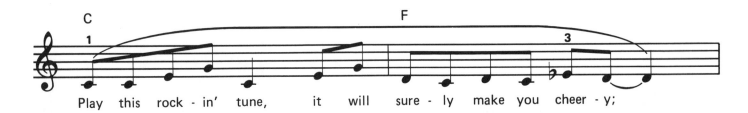

When you feel in trou - ble, just   rock   it   a - way!

It is often very effective to play pairs of eighth notes with a swinging "lilt." That is, with the first eighth a little longer than its value and the 2nd a little shorter:

long   short, long   short, etc.

This is a good piece to try this on.

Try this piece with VARIATION added, if available. Also try with other Rhythms, such as ROCK 'N' ROLL, POP, SHUFFLE, etc.

Measuring Half Steps & Whole Steps

Half Steps

A **HALF STEP** is the distance from any key to the very next key above or below (black or white).

HALF STEPS • NO KEY BETWEEN

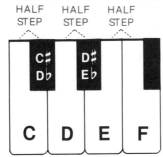

Whole Steps

A **WHOLE STEP** is equal to 2 half steps. Skip one key (black or white).

WHOLE STEPS • ONE KEY BETWEEN

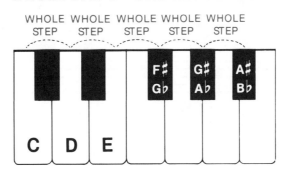

Tetrachords

A **TETRACHORD** is a series of **FOUR NOTES** having a pattern of
WHOLE STEP, WHOLE STEP, HALF STEP.

The notes of a tetrachord must be in alphabetical order →

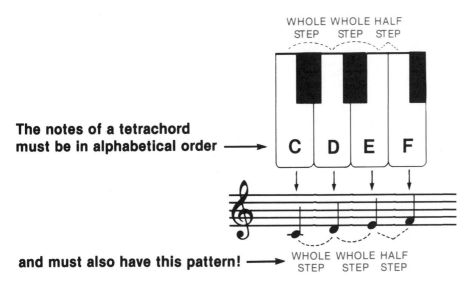

and must also have this pattern! →

The Major Scale

The MAJOR SCALE is made of **TWO TETRACHORDS** *joined* by a **WHOLE STEP**.

The C MAJOR SCALE is constructed as follows:

> There is NO ♯ OR ♭
> in the **C MAJOR SCALE.**

Each scale begins and ends on a note of the same name as the scale, called the **KEY NOTE**.

Preparation for Scale Playing

IMPORTANT!   Since there are **EIGHT** notes in the C MAJOR SCALE and we have only **FIVE** fingers, an important trick must be mastered: **crossing the thumb under the 3rd finger!** This exercise will make this trick easy.

Play HANDS SEPARATELY. Begin VERY SLOWLY. Keep the wrist loose and quiet!

Auto: OFF   **Rhythm:** OFF   **Register:** PIANO   **Sustain:** ON

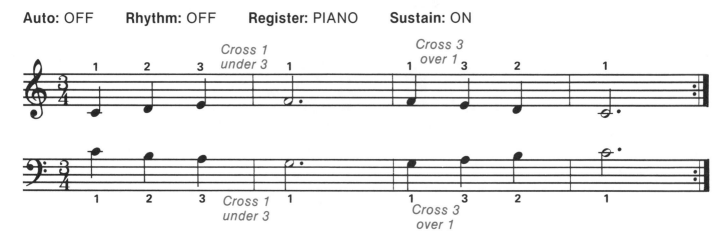

The C Major Scale

Begin SLOWLY. **Lean** the hand slightly in the direction you are moving. The hand should move smoothly along with no twisting motion of the wrist!

Auto: OFF   **Rhythm:** OFF   **Register:** PIANO   **Sustain:** ON

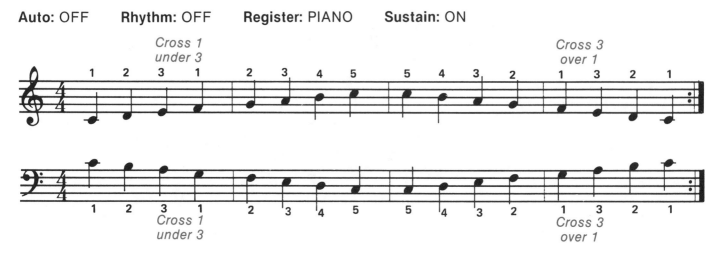

JOY TO THE WORLD!

This well-known piece is made up almost entirely of scales. This version is played with *Auto OFF*, so the entire keyboard will be used like an organ or piano, and you will have the opportunity to play and hear the C MAJOR SCALE with each hand separately.

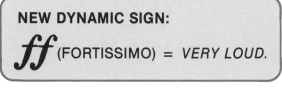

NEW DYNAMIC SIGN:

ff (FORTISSIMO) = *VERY LOUD.*

Auto: OFF   **Register:** ORGAN or TRUMPET with Sustain OFF, or
Rhythm: OFF   PIANO with Sustain ON

G.F. Handel

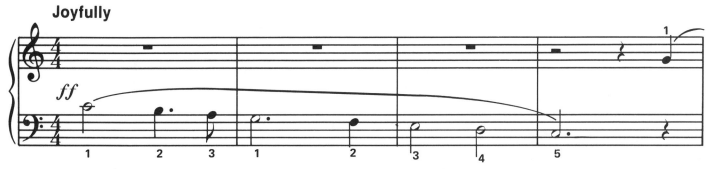

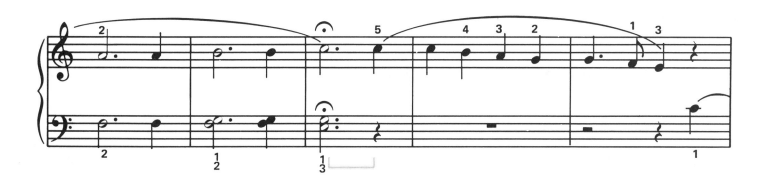

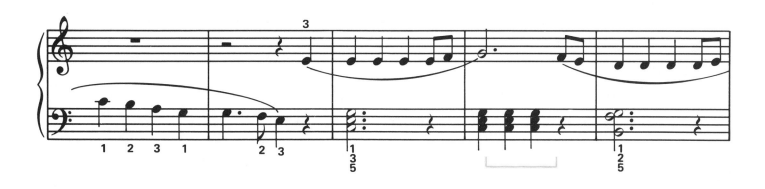

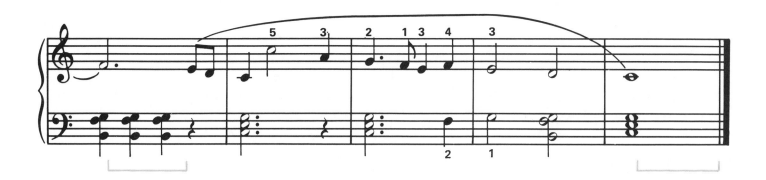

More About Chords

A TRIAD IS A 3-NOTE CHORD.

THE THREE NOTES OF A TRIAD ARE:

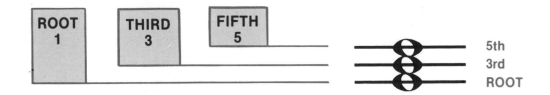

The ROOT is the note from which the triad gets its name. The ROOT of a C triad is C.

TRIADS IN **ROOT POSITION** (WITH ROOT AT THE BOTTOM)
ALWAYS LOOK LIKE THIS:

TRIADS MAY BE BUILT ON ANY NOTE OF ANY SCALE.

TRIADS IN C

Play with RH

Auto: OFF   **Register:** PIANO
Rhythm: OFF   **Sustain:** ON

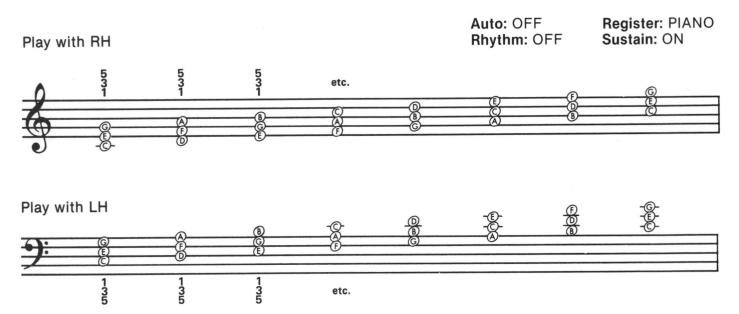

LISTEN CAREFULLY TO THE SOUND OF THESE ROOT POSITION TRIADS!

When you name the notes of any **TRIAD IN ROOT POSITION,** you will always skip **ONE** letter of the musical alphabet between each note. The triads you played above are:

C E G   D F A   E G B   F A C   G B D   A C E   B D F

This is the complete **"TRIAD VOCABULARY!"** It should be memorized!

COCKLES AND MUSSELS

This piece, which contains NO SHARPS & NO FLATS, is in the **KEY OF C MAJOR.**

Play the LH alone at first, saying the names of the notes of each triad aloud.
Begin with the LOWEST note of each triad.

KEY OF C MAJOR
Key Signature: no ♯, no ♭.

Auto: OFF   **Register:** GUITAR or PIANO
Rhythm: OFF   **Sustain:** ON

The Primary Chords in C Major

The 3 most important chords in any key are those built on the 1st, 4th, & 5th notes of the scale. These are called the **PRIMARY CHORDS** of the key.

The chords are identified by the Roman numerals **I, IV, & V** (1, 4, & 5).
The **V** chord usually adds the note a 7th above the root to make a **V7** (5-7) chord.

In the key of C MAJOR, the **I CHORD** is the C MAJOR TRIAD.
The **IV CHORD** is the F MAJOR TRIAD.
The **V7 CHORD** is the G7 CHORD (G major triad with an added 7th).

THE PRIMARY CHORDS IN C MAJOR:

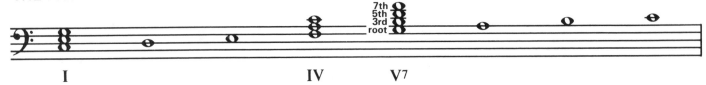

Chord Progressions

When we change from one chord to another, we call this a "CHORD PROGRESSION."

When all chords are in root position, the hand must leap from one chord to the next. To make the chord progressions easier to play and sound better, the IV and V7 chords may be played in other positions by moving one or more of the higher chord tones down an octave.

The I chord
is played in
ROOT POSITION:

The top note of the
IV chord is moved
down an octave:

In the V7 chord, the 5th (D)
is usually omitted.

All notes except the root
are moved down an octave.

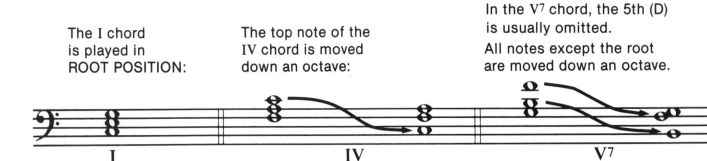

The 3 PRIMARY CHORDS are then
comfortably played as follows:

| **Auto:** OFF | **Register:** PIANO |
| **Rhythm:** OFF | **Sustain:** ON |

It is important that you now think
of the C, F & G7 chords in the key
of C MAJOR as the I, IV & V7 chords!

Play the following line several times,
saying the numerals of each chord as you play.

| **Auto:** OFF | **Register:** PIANO |
| **Rhythm:** OFF | **Sustain:** ON |

About the Blues

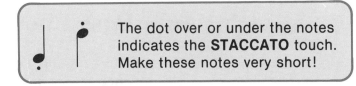

The dot over or under the notes indicates the **STACCATO** touch. Make these notes very short!

Music called BLUES has long been a part of the American musical heritage. We find it in the music of many popular song writers, in ballads, boogie, and rock.

BLUES music follows a basic formula, that is, a standard chord progression. If you learn the formula for *GOT THOSE BLUES!* you will be able to play the blues in any key you learn, simply by applying the formula to that key.

FORMULA FOR THE BLUES:

There are 12 measures in one "chorus" of the blues:

4 measures of the I chord; 2 measures of the IV chord; 2 measures of the I chord;
1 measure of the V⁷ chord; 1 measure of the IV chord; 2 measures of the I chord.

GOT THOSE BLUES!

The eighth notes may be played a bit unevenly: long   short,   long   short, etc.

The Blues, with Auto Bass Chord & Rhythm

Now use the following setting: **Auto:** ON "Single Finger"
Rhythm: Moderately slow SWING or SLOW ROCK

You will see that it is fun to play the LH alone, using the standard BLUES progression.
Count "1-2-3-4" for each measure. Each slash mark (✏) represents ONE count.
Press SYNCHRO and play.

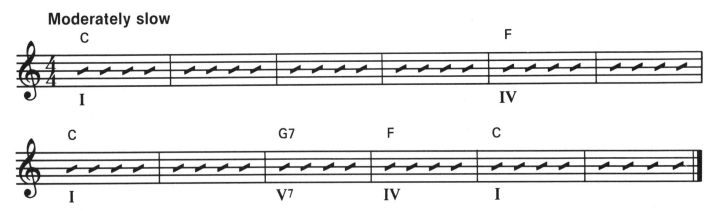

Repeat the above, adding VARIATION or other special effects.

GOT THOSE BLUES!

Play with one of the above settings. **Choose your own Register.**
To make the *ritardando* at the end, gradually slow the tempo down, using your tempo control.
The Rhythm will continue to play, slower and slower.

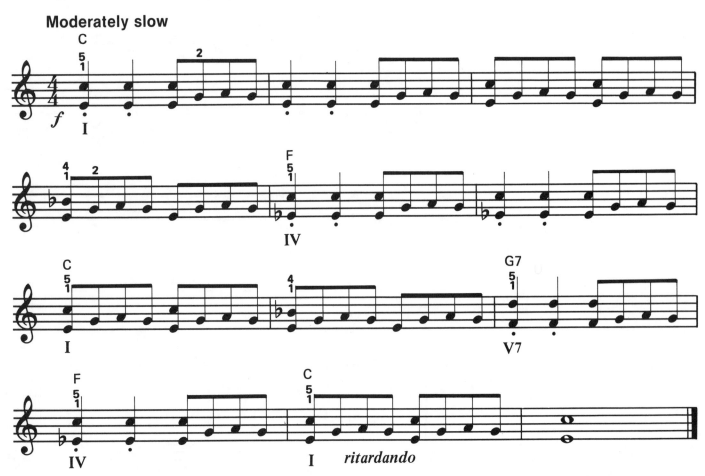

NOTE: The BLUES works well with almost any Rhythm, except WALTZ or LATIN rhythms.
Try *GOT THOSE BLUES* with other Rhythms and various effects.

RH: An Extended Position

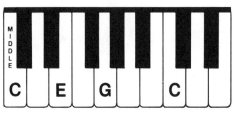

ON TOP OF OLD SMOKY begins and ends with the RH in an EXTENDED POSITION.

Play several times:
Register: PIANO
Sustain: ON

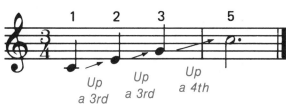

Up a 3rd   Up a 3rd   Up a 4th

ON TOP OF OLD SMOKY

Auto: ON "Single Finger"
Rhythm: Moderate WALTZ
Register: PIANO, VIBES or MUSIC BOX
Sustain: ON

1. Play RH alone without Rhythm. Count aloud.
2. Add LH: Press SYNCHRO, then begin.
   Play the first LH F only when the letter F apears above the RH note
   (on the first syllable of the word "Smoky")!
3. Play again, adding VARIATION or ARPEGGIOS, DUET and other effects.

KEY OF C MAJOR
Key Signature: no ♯, no ♭.

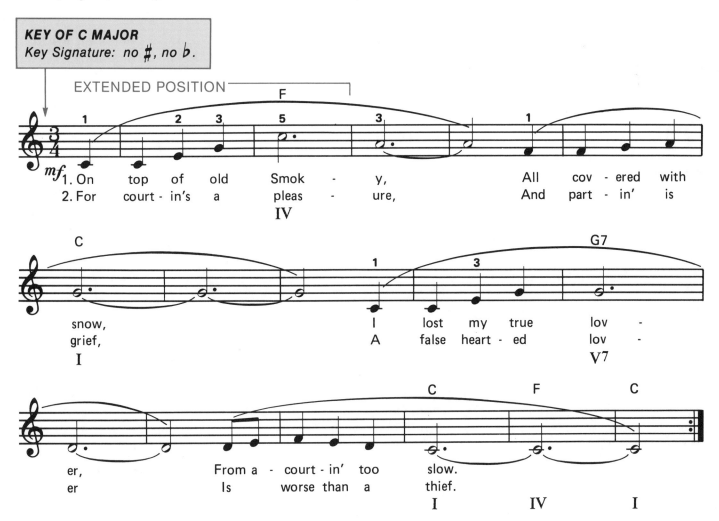

The G Major Scale

Remember that the MAJOR SCALE is made up of two tetrachords *joined* by a whole step.
The 2nd TETRACHORD of the G MAJOR SCALE begins on D.

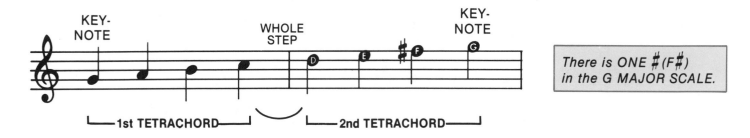

There is ONE ♯ (F♯)
in the G MAJOR SCALE.

The Key of G Major

A piece based on the G Major scale is in the **KEY OF G MAJOR.**
Since F is sharp in the G scale, every F will be sharp in the key of G Major.

Instead of placing a sharp before every F in the entire piece,
the sharp is indicated at the beginning in the KEY SIGNATURE.

Practice the G MAJOR SCALE with HANDS SEPARATE.
Begin SLOWLY. Keep the wrist loose and quiet.

KEY OF G MAJOR
Key Signature: one sharp (F♯)
Play all "F's" sharp throughout.

Auto: OFF **Register:** PIANO
Rhythm: OFF **Sustain:** ON

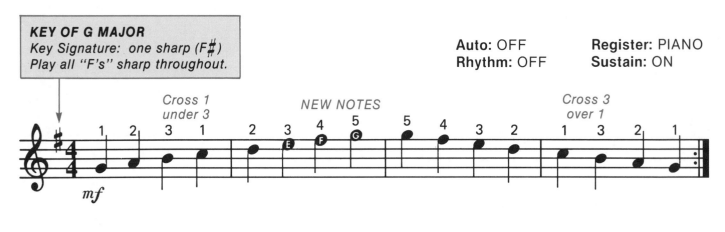

IMPORTANT! After you have learned the G MAJOR SCALE with hands separate, you may play the hands together. When the scale is played as written on the staffs above, the LH descends as the RH ascends, and vice versa. This is called CONTRARY MOTION—both hands play the SAME NUMBERED fingers at the same time!

You may also play, the C MAJOR SCALE at the bottom of page 66 with the hands together, in CONTRARY MOTION!

A New Trick!

CHANGING FINGERS ON THE SAME NOTE: Sometimes it is necessary to replay the same note with a different finger. Practice the following line to prepare for *THE CAN-CAN.*

Auto: OFF   **Rhythm:** OFF   **Register:** TRUMPET   **Sustain:** OFF

The Can-Can

Auto: ON "Single Finger"
Rhythm: Slow MARCH, or moderately fast SWING or POP

Register: TRUMPET
Sustain: OFF

1. Play RH alone without Rhythm. Count aloud.
2. Add Rhythm.
3. Add LH: Press SYNCHRO, then begin.
4. Try other Registers and additional effects, if you wish.

KEY OF G MAJOR
Key Signature: one sharp (F♯)

J. Offenbach

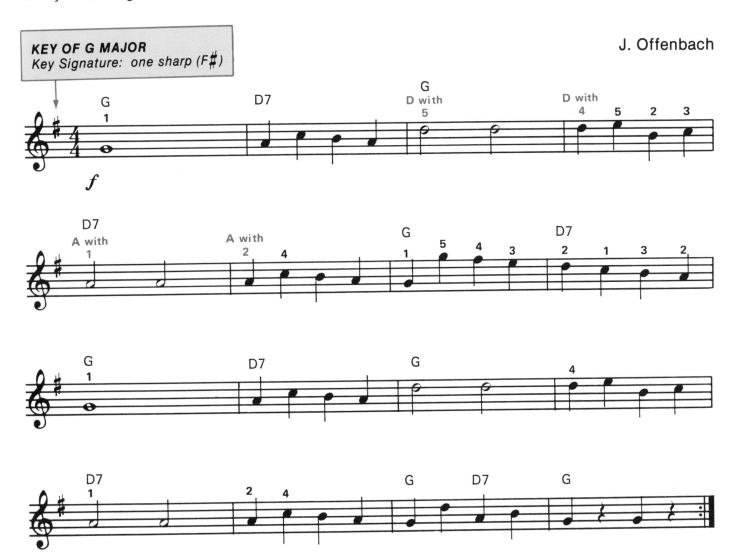

The Primary Chords in G Major

Reviewing the G MAJOR SCALE, LH ascending.

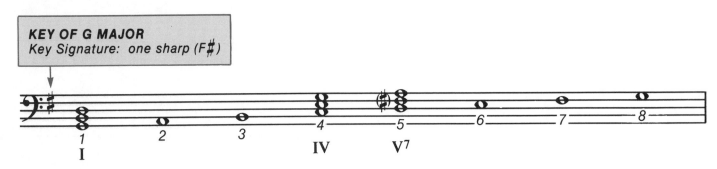

The following chord positions
(which you have already learned)
are used for smooth progressions:

Auto: ON "Fingered Chord"   **Rhythm:** OFF

Primary Chords in G

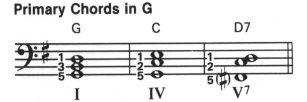

G Major Chord Progression with I, IV, & V7 Chords.
Play several times, saying the numerals aloud:

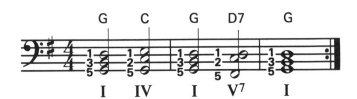

THE MARINES' HYMN

Auto: ON "Fingered Chord"   **Rhythm:** OFF   **Register:** ORGAN or TRUMPET   **Sustain:** OFF

1. Play RH alone.
2. Add LH.
3. Add slow MARCH or moderately fast SWING or POP rhythm. Press SYNCHRO,
   then play hands together.
4. OPTIONAL: Play again with "Single Finger" chords.

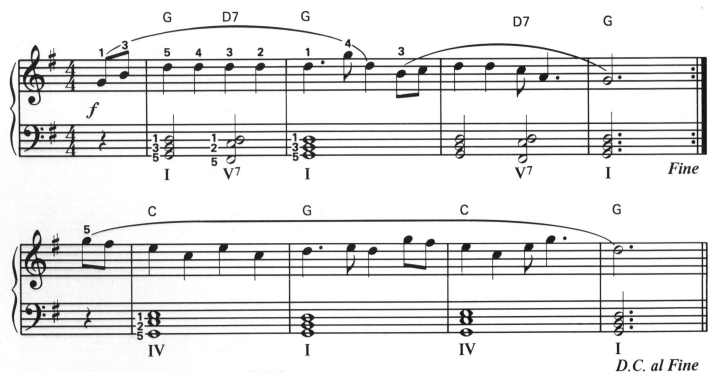

Press STOP button at the end, or FADE.

WHY AM I BLUE?

> The NATURAL sign ♮ cancels a sharp or flat!
> A note after a NATURAL SIGN is always a WHITE KEY!

Auto: ON "Single Finger"
Rhythm: Moderately slow SLOW ROCK

Register: PIANO with Sustain ON, or
TRUMPET with Sustain OFF

1. Play RH alone without Rhythm.
2. Add Rhythm.
3. Add LH: Press SYNCHRO, then begin.
4. Add DUET, if available.

KEY OF G MAJOR
Key Signature: one sharp (F♯)

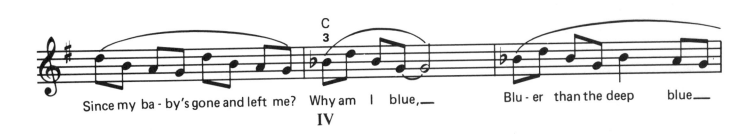

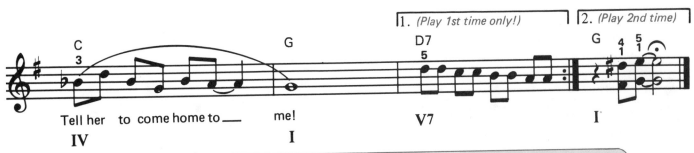

> To end this piece, use the LH to slow down the tempo while you hold the last RH notes (under the fermata), then gradually turn down the MASTER VOLUME.

5. OPTIONAL: Play *WHY AM I BLUE* with "Fingered Chords." Use the same settings.
   Add VARIATION and/or other effects.

The F Major Scale

There is ONE ♭ (B♭) in the F MAJOR SCALE.

The fingering for the F MAJOR SCALE with the LH is the same as for all the scales you have studied so far: 5 4 3 2 1 - 3 2 1 ascending; 1 2 3 - 1 2 3 4 5 descending.

Play slowly and carefully!

KEY OF F MAJOR
Key Signature: 1 flat (B♭)

Auto: OFF **Register:** PIANO
Rhythm: OFF **Sustain:** ON

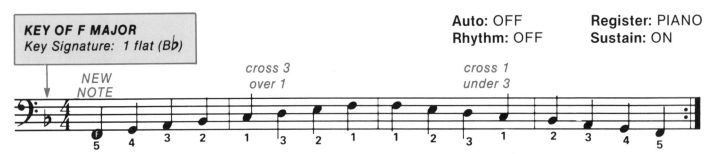

To play the F MAJOR SCALE with the RH, the 5th finger is not used! The fingers fall in the following groups: 1 2 3 4 - 1 2 3 4 ascending; 4 3 2 1 - 4 3 2 1 descending.

Play slowly and carefully!

As soon as you play the thumb, move it under, carrying it at the base of the 3rd and 4th fingers until it is needed. Keep the wrist even, and move the hand smoothly along. Never twist the wrist when the thumb goes under.

Begin slowly and gradually increase speed. Play several times daily.

Play only with HANDS SEPARATE:

LITTLE BROWN JUG

Auto: OFF **Rhythm:** OFF **Register:** PIANO, GUITAR, or ORGAN **Sustain:** OFF

1. Play RH alone.
2. Play LH alone.
3. Play hands together.
4. Add Rhythm. Use slow MARCH or moderately slow SWING.

IMPORTANT! You will enjoy playing *LITTLE BROWN JUG* again, using the "Single Finger" chord setting. The chord names are above the music. Make the Bb MAJOR CHORD by playing Bb with the 2nd finger.

The Primary Chords in F Major

Reviewing the F MAJOR SCALE, LH ascending.

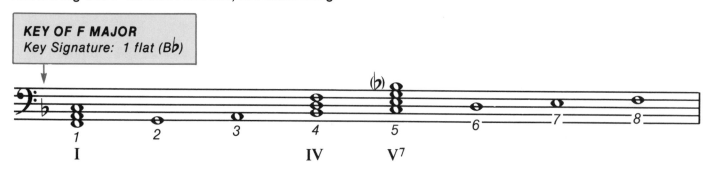

KEY OF F MAJOR
Key Signature: 1 flat (Bb)

The following positions are often used,
for smooth progressions:

Auto: OFF   **Register:** PIANO
Rhythm: OFF   **Sustain:** ON

Primary Chords in F

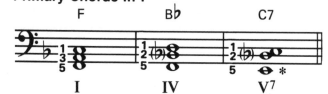

F Major Chord Progression with I, IV, V7 Chords.

Play several times, saying the chord names
and numerals aloud:

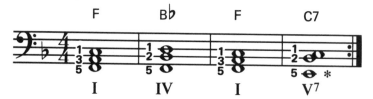

CHIAPANECAS *(Mexican Hand-Clapping Song)*

1. Play RH alone.
2. Add LH.
3. Add moderately fast WALTZ rhythm. Press SYNCHRO, then play hands together.

Auto: ON "Fingered Chord"   **Register:** ORGAN
Rhythm: OFF   **Sustain:** OFF

IMPORTANT: When the "Fingered Chord" setting is used with Rhythm, you will not hear the chords sustained. They will sound in the Rhythm, on the 2nd and 3rd counts of each measure. Also, you need not hold each chord. Just play the chord and release it. The same harmony will continue until you play the next chord.

KEY OF F MAJOR
Key Signature: 1 flat (Bb)

*If the low "E" is not on your instrument, it may be omitted.

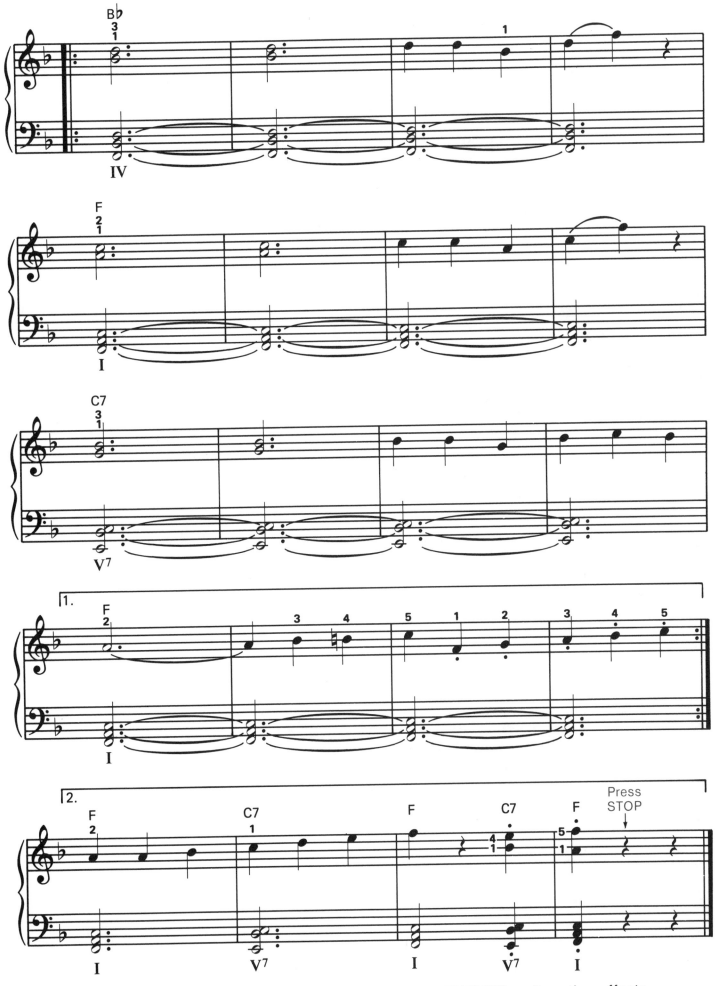

4. Play *CHIAPANECAS* again, adding DUET, VARIATION or ARPEGGIO and/or other effects.
5. Play *CHIAPANECAS* using "Single Finger" chords. For the B♭ MAJOR CHORD, play B♭ with the 2nd finger.

HE'S GOT THE WHOLE WORLD IN HIS HANDS

Auto: ON "Single Finger"　　　　**Register:** ORGAN, SAX or SYNTHE
Rhythm: Moderately fast SHUFFLE　　**Sustain:** OFF

This is a great piece to play with SHUFFLE rhythm. If you do not have this,
substitute POP, SLOW ROCK, or ROCK 'N' ROLL.

1. Play RH alone, without Rhythm.
2. Add LH: Press SYNCHRO, then begin.
3. Add DUET, VARIATION or ARPEGGIO and/or other effects.

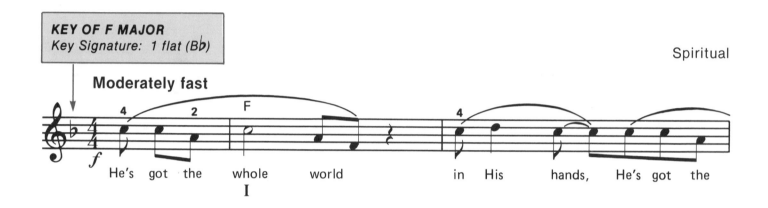

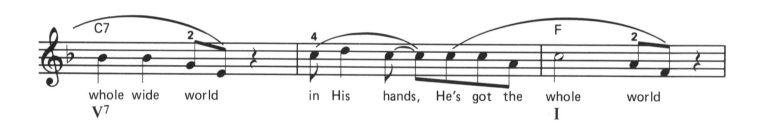

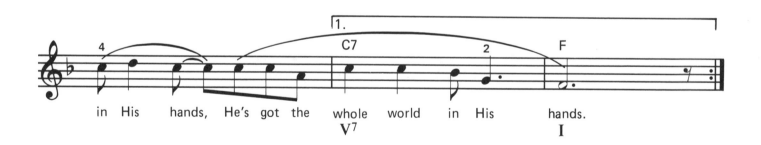

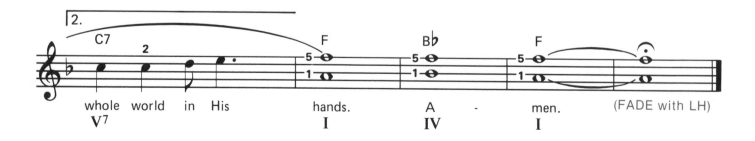

4. OPTIONAL: Play again using "Fingered Chords."

DOWN IN THE VALLEY

Auto: ON "Single Finger"
Rhythm: Moderately slow WALTZ
Register: PIANO or GUITAR
Sustain: ON

1. Play RH alone, without Rhythm.
2. Add LH: Press SYNCHRO, then begin.
3. Add DUET and VARIATION or ARPEGGIO, if available.

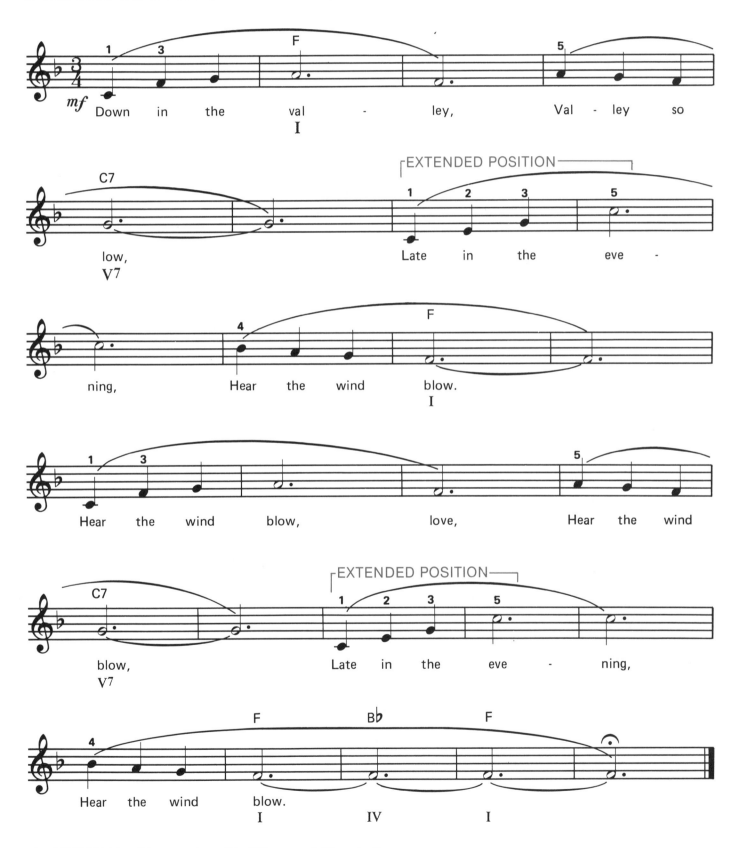

4. OPTIONAL: Play again with "Fingered Chords."

The Key of A Minor (Relative of C Major)

Every MAJOR KEY has a RELATIVE MINOR KEY that has the same KEY SIGNATURE.

The RELATIVE MINOR begins on the 6th TONE of the MAJOR SCALE.

The RELATIVE MINOR of C MAJOR is, therefore, A MINOR.

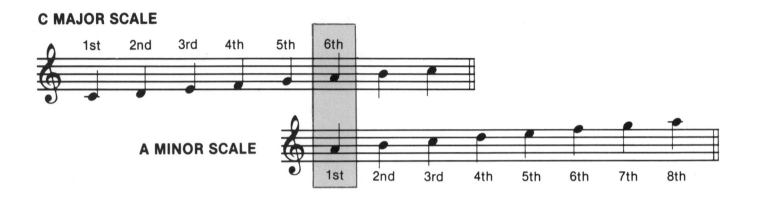

Because the keys of C MAJOR & A MINOR have the same KEY SIGNATURE (no ♯'s, no ♭'s), they are RELATIVES.

The minor scale shown above is called the NATURAL MINOR SCALE. It uses only notes that are found in the relative major scale.

The A Harmonic Minor Scale

The MOST FREQUENTLY USED MINOR SCALE is the HARMONIC MINOR. In this scale, the 7th tone is raised ascending and descending.

The raised 7th in the key of A MINOR is G♯. It is not included in the key signature, but is written in as an "accidental" sharp each time it occurs.

Practice the A HARMONIC MINOR SCALE with HANDS SEPARATE. Begin slowly.

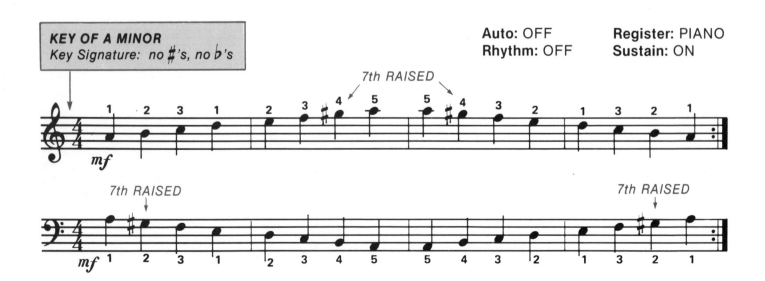

MORE SYNCOPATED NOTES:

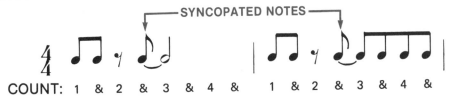

See how many syncopated notes you can find in *JERICHO.*

JERICHO

Auto: OFF   **Rhythm:** Moderate SWING, ROCK or POP   **Register:** ORGAN   **Sustain:** ON

1. Play RH alone without Rhythm. Count aloud.
2. Add Rhythm. Be sure to check tempo before playing.
3. Practice LH alone, slowly. Count aloud. If your instrument does not have the low E, you may ignore it.
4. Play hands together: Press SYNCHRO and begin. Rhythm will begin when you play the LH keys.

More About Triads

1. Some of the 3rds you have been playing are MAJOR 3rds, and some are MINOR (smaller) 3rds.

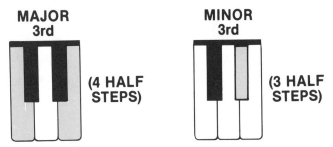

MAJOR 3rd (4 HALF STEPS) **MINOR 3rd** (3 HALF STEPS)

Any MAJOR 3rd may be changed to a MINOR 3rd by lowering the UPPER NOTE ½ step!

2. All of the 5ths you have played so far are PERFECT 5ths.

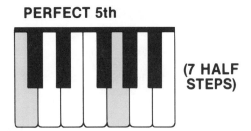

PERFECT 5th (7 HALF STEPS)

3. MAJOR TRIADS consist of a ROOT, MAJOR 3rd, & PERFECT 5th.

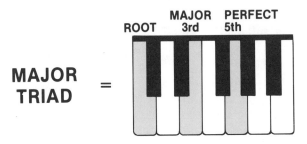

MAJOR TRIAD = ROOT, MAJOR 3rd, PERFECT 5th

4. MINOR TRIADS consist of a ROOT, MINOR 3rd, & PERFECT 5th.

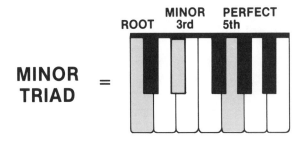

MINOR TRIAD = ROOT, MINOR 3rd, PERFECT 5th

Any MAJOR TRIAD may be changed to a MINOR TRIAD by lowering the 3rd one half step!

5. Play the following triads with LH 5 3 1. Say "F MAJOR TRIAD, F MINOR TRIAD," etc., as you play each pair.

Auto: ON "Fingered Chord"

The Primary Chords in A Minor

Reviewing the A HARMONIC MINOR SCALE, LH ascending.
Small lower case Roman numerals are used to indicate minor triads (**i** & **iv**).
(Small m = minor.)

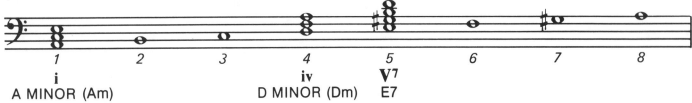

i   iv   V⁷
A MINOR (Am)   D MINOR (Dm)   E7

Auto: OFF   **Rhythm:** OFF   **Register:** PIANO   **Sustain:** ON

The following positions are often used, for smooth progressions.

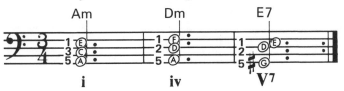

MINOR EVENT

Auto: OFF   **Rhythm:** OFF   **Register:** ORGAN   **Sustain:** OFF

1. Play hands separately. Ignore last 3 measures. Count aloud.

2. Play hands together. Ignore last 3 measures.

3. Change to the following setting:

    Auto: ON "Fingered Chord"   **Register:** ORGAN with Sustain OFF, or
    Rhythm: Moderately fast SWING   PIANO with Sustain ON

4. Play hands together. Use SYNCHRO. Include the last 3 measures and gradually slow the tempo with RH in the next to last measure. In the last measure HOLD the **Am** chord while you press the STOP button.

5. Play again, adding VARIATION or ARPEGGIO, DUET and other effects.

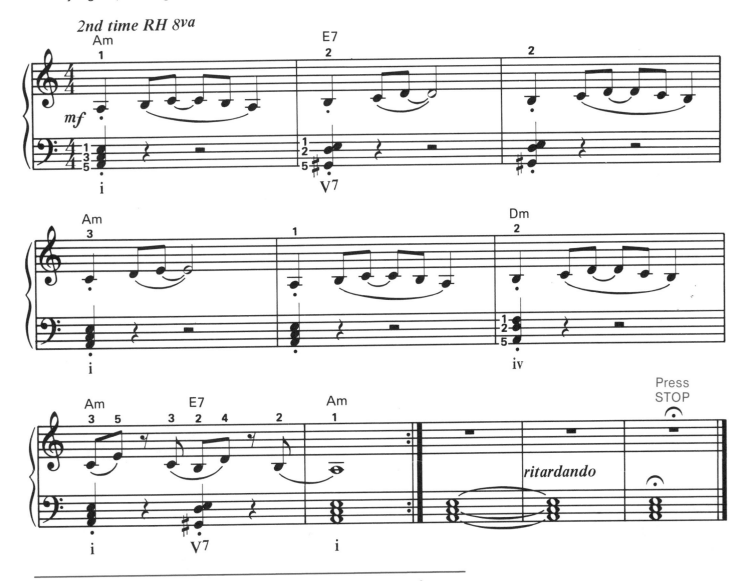

Experimenting with Fancy Rhythms

This piece adapts itself to any rhythm except WALTZ. Your instrument probably has some of the following rhythms: SHUFFLE, BOSSA NOVA, SAMBA, RHUMBA, TANGO, LATIN SWING, BEGUINE, DISCO, 16 BEAT, etc.

Select one of the rhythms listed above. Play *MINOR EVENT* again, keeping the SAME TEMPO SETTING. Include VARIATION, DUET, VIBRATO, STEREO and other effects you like. Press SYNCHRO and begin.

Do not let any of the fancy beats you hear distract you. Counting aloud at first will help. You will see how different this piece sounds with each one of these more intricate rhythms.

How to Play "Single Finger" Minor Chords

The "Single Finger" minor chord requires 2 fingers to play.

On almost ALL makes other than YAMAHA,
the minor chord is played as follows:

Play the KEY NOTE plus any KEY to the RIGHT, BLACK or WHITE.
It is easiest to simply add the *very next* WHITE KEY to the RIGHT.

For A minor, play A and B together. Use the 3rd and 2nd fingers.

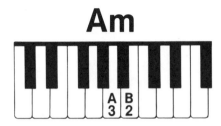

On YAMAHA instruments, the minor chord is played as follows:

Play the KEY NOTE plus any BLACK KEY to the LEFT.
It is easiest to simply add the *very next* BLACK KEY to the LEFT.

For A minor, play A♭ and A together. Use the 3rd and 2nd fingers.

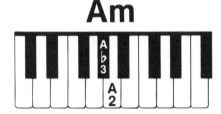

> **IMPORTANT!** On a few makes of instruments the minor chord is formed in other ways.
> **PLEASE CONSULT YOUR OWNER'S MANUAL.**

JERICHO with "Single Finger" Chords

Auto: ON "Single Finger"   **Register:** ORGAN or TRUMPET
Rhythm: Moderately fast SWING   **Sustain:** OFF

1. Press SYNCHRO and play hands together. Press STOP on the 1st count of the last measure, even if you must release the tied note to do it. Play the **Am** chord again on the last note.

2. Add VARIATION, DUET and/or other effects.

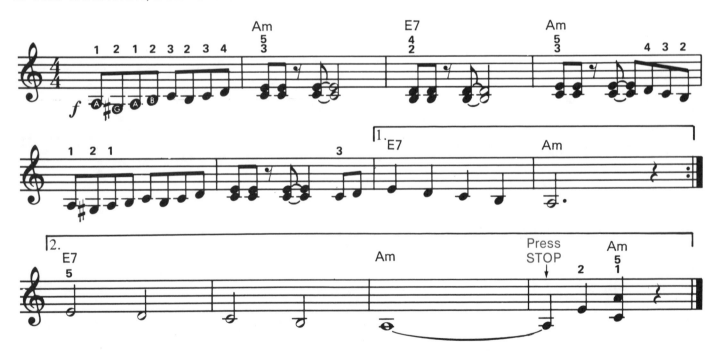

3. Play again with some of the more intricate rhythms, such as RHUMBA, 16 BEAT, or others of your choice. Some rhythms work better when the eighth notes are played unevenly (long-short).

4. OPTIONAL: Play *JERICHO* with "Fingered Chord" setting, forming your own LH chords.

GREENSLEEVES

Auto: ON "Single Finger" **Register:** Choose your own
Rhythm: Moderately slow WALTZ **Sustain:** Acceptable with certain registers. Experiment!

1. Play RH alone. Use Rhythm, if you wish.
2. Add LH: Press SYNCHRO and begin.
3. Add VARIATION or ARPEGGIO. Also DUET, if available, along with other effects.

*Play this A minor chord on the 3rd count. Play it firmly, and do not be late!
**FINGER SUBSTITUTION: While holding the note down with 1, change to 3 on the 2nd beat.

ROCK-A MY SOUL

REVIEWING THE KEY OF C MAJOR

Auto: ON "Single Finger"
Rhythm: Moderately slow SHUFFLE, SWING or POP

Register: ORGAN or SYNTHE with Sustain OFF,
or PIANO with Sustain ON

1. Play RH alone, without Rhythm.
   Play eighth notes unevenly, with a swing, long-short.
2. Add LH: Press SYNCHRO, then begin.
3. Add DUET, VARIATON and/or other effects on the repeat, if you wish.
   (See 1st ending and footnote.)

Rock - a my soul in the bos - om of A - bra - ham,

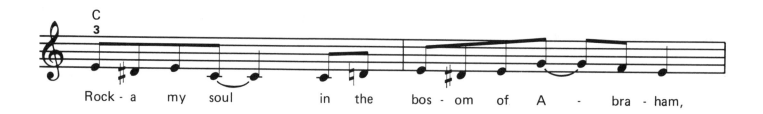

Rock - a my soul in the bos - om of A - bra - ham,

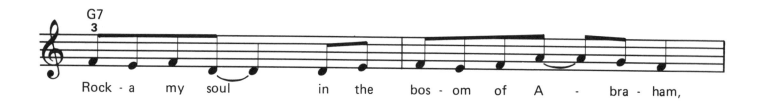

Rock - a my soul in the bos - om of A - bra - ham,

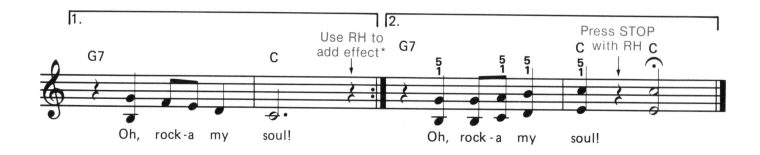

Oh, rock - a my soul!   Oh, rock - a my soul!

*Here the RH can add VARIATION, DUET, or any other effect available, on the rest.

THE ENTERTAINER

Auto: ON "Single Finger"
Rhythm: Moderately slow SWING

Register: ORGAN or SYNTHE with Sustain OFF, or
PIANO with Sustain ON

1. Play RH alone, slowly, without Rhythm.
2. Add Rhythm: Press START, adjust tempo, listen to a few measures, counting "1-2-3-4,"
   then play RH again, beginning on the 4th count.
3. Add LH: Press SYNCHRO, then begin.
4. Add DUET, if available.

Scott Joplin

Eighth Note Triplets

When three notes are grouped together with a figure "*3*" above or below the notes, the group is called a **TRIPLET.**

The THREE NOTES of an
EIGHTH NOTE TRIPLET GROUP = ONE QUARTER NOTE.

When a piece contains triplets, count "TRIP-A-LET"
or "ONE & THEN"
or any way suggested by your teacher.

AMAZING GRACE

Auto: ON "Single Finger"   **Rhythm:** Moderately slow WALTZ   **Register:** PIANO   **Sustain:** ON

1. Play RH alone, very slowly, without Rhythm.
2. Add Rhythm: Press START, adjust tempo, listen to a few measures, counting "1-2-3,"
   then play RH again, beginning on the 3rd count.
3. Add LH: Press SYNCHRO, then begin.
4. Add VARIATION or ARPEGGIO, plus other effects.

John Newton, J. Carrell, & D. Clayton

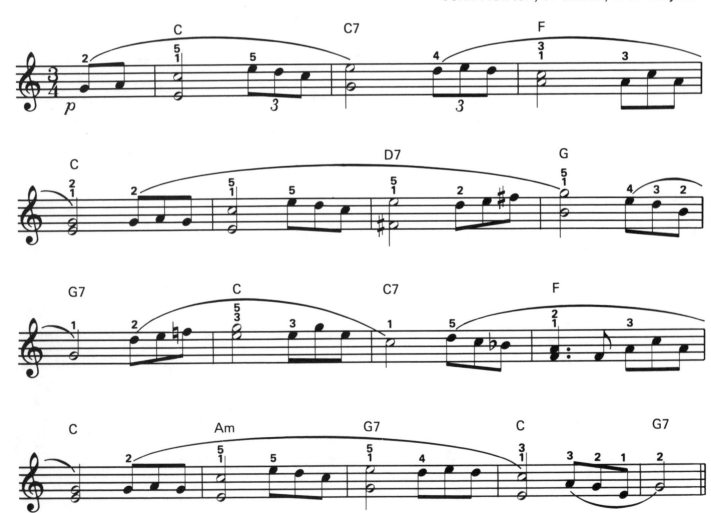

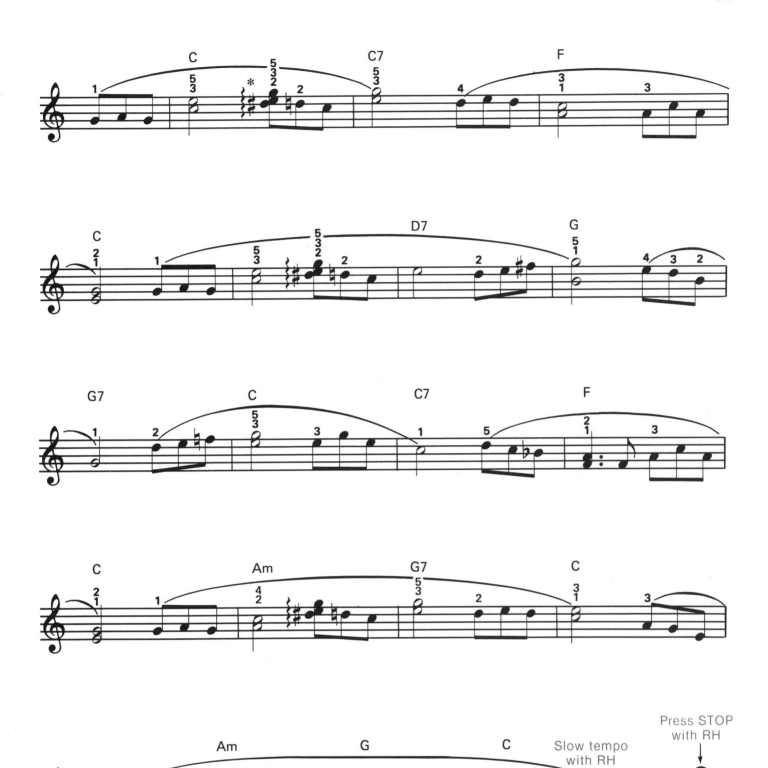

ARPEGGIATED CHORDS

When a wavy line appears beside the chord, the chord is *arpeggiated* (broken or rolled). Play the lowest note first, and quickly add the higher notes one at a time until the chord is complete. The first note is played on the beat.

Improvising in the DORIAN MODE★

by THOMAS M. PALMER

Anyone can improvise a modern sounding piece by following these simple directions:

1. Use **Auto:** ON "Single Finger" **Register:** ORGAN
   Rhythm: Moderately fast SWING **Sustain:** OFF

2. Play the LH notes that make the D MINOR CHORD (abbreviated "Dm").
   On most instruments, play D & E together, with LH 3 2. (See Owner's Manual.)
   On YAMAHA instruments, play D♭ and D together, with LH 3 2.

4. Press SYNCHRO, play **Dm** and let the instrument play a few measures.

5. With RH play ANYTHING you wish, using only WHITE KEYS. You may play keys in ANY order, and in any rhythm. Later you may wish to try other registers and experiment with Sustain ON or OFF. Add VARIATION, DUET, etc., if you wish.

The following will serve as an example. It keeps the RH in the same five-finger position throughout, with the thumb on D.

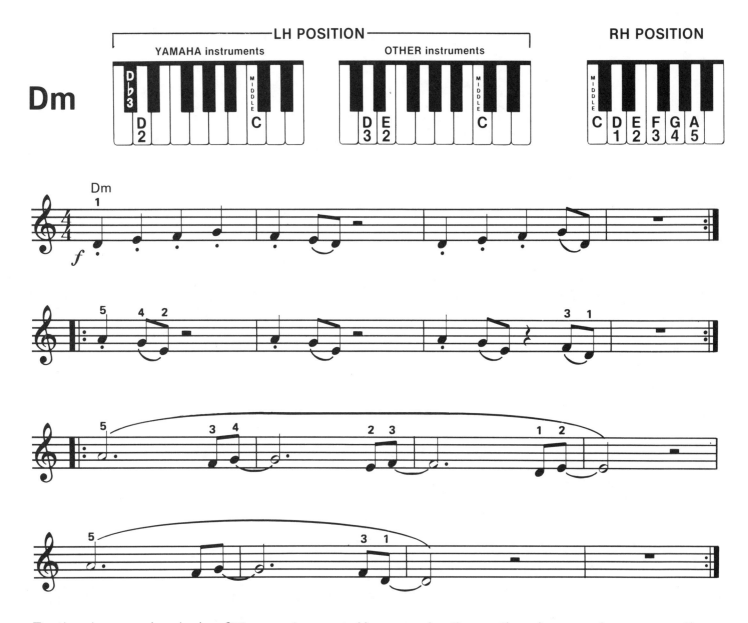

Try the above again, playing *8va* on each repeat. You may play the sections in any order, as many times as you wish. End anywhere you like, and FADE by turning down the MASTER VOLUME and the RHYTHM VOLUME with the LH.

★Pieces using all WHITE KEYS with Dm are not in any key, but are in an ancient MODE, called the DORIAN MODE. The DORIAN MODE is used by many popular rock groups.

Getting Rid of Your Inhibitions

The beginning of each of the following two lines of music will prove that ANY white note will sound good against the LH Dm chord. In improvising, you must feel absolutely free to play ANY note you choose. In DORIAN MODE, any white note is a good choice.

Auto: ON "Single Finger"   **Rhythm:** Moderately fast SWING   **Register:** OPTIONAL

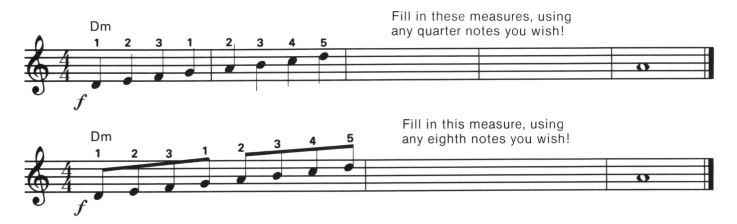

Fill in these measures, using
any quarter notes you wish!

Fill in this measure, using
any eighth notes you wish!

Adding GRACE NOTES

Small notes called "GRACE NOTES" (♪) are often used to "embellish" or decorate improvisations to make the ideas more effective.

Grace notes have no definite time value. They are played VERY QUICKLY, almost at the same time as the following large note.

Grace notes are easily added to the first note of an idea or pattern. Here is an example of an idea to which grace notes may be added. Notice that the small notes are one half-step below the note they embellish, and that black notes may be used in the Dorian mode, if they move quickly to a white note.

Same, with grace notes added:

IMPORTANT!! Play the improvisation on page 94 again, adding grace notes to the first note of each line, and at the beginning of similar patterns when they repeat, such as on the 1st note of the 3rd measure of the 1st line, and the 1st note of the 2nd and 3rd measures of the 2nd line.

The first idea may be fingered as follows:

Fingered Chord Chart

With this chart you can form your own chords from individual notes, for use with Auto OFF or Auto ON "Fingered Chord."

The chords most used in popular music are given here in their ROOT POSITIONS. If you are using Auto ON "Fingered Chord," the chord may not fit in the accompaniment section in this position. When this is the case, move the top note of the chord down one octave.

For example, the B♭7 chord is B♭ D F A♭. The A♭ is out of the range of the accompaniment section. To play this chord with the "Fingered Chord" setting, move the A♭ down one octave, and play A♭ B♭ D F.

ROOT	MAJOR	MINOR (m)	SEVENTH (7)	DIMINISHED (dim or °)	AUGMENTED (aug or +)	MAJOR 7th (M7)	MINOR 7th (m7)
A	A C♯ E	A C E	A C♯ E G	A C E♭ G♭	A C♯ E♯ (F)	A C♯ E G♯	A C E G
B♭	B♭ D F	B♭ D♭ F	B♭ D F A♭	B♭ D♭ F♭ A♭♭ (E) (G)	B♭ D F♯	B♭ D F A	B♭ D♭ F A♭
B	B D♯ F♯	B D F♯	B D♯ F♯ A	B D F A♭	B D♯ F𝄪 (G)	B D♯ F♯ A♯	B D F♯ A
C	C E G	C E♭ G	C E G B♭	C E♭ G♭ B♭♭ (A)	C E G♯	C E G B	C E♭ G B♭
D♭	D♭ F A♭	D♭ F♭ A♭ (E)	D♭ F A♭ C♭ (B)	D♭ F♭ A♭♭ C♭♭ (E) (G) (B♭)	D♭ F A	D♭ F A♭ C	D♭ F♭ A♭ C♭ (E) (B)
D	D F♯ A	D F A	D F♯ A C	D F A♭ C♭ (B)	D F♯ A♯	D F♯ A C♯	D F A C
E♭	E♭ G B♭	E♭ G♭ B♭	E♭ G B♭ D♭	E♭ G♭ B♭♭ D♭♭ (A) (C)	E♭ G B	E♭ G B♭ D	E♭ G♭ B♭ D♭
E	E G♯ B	E G B	E G♯ B D	E G B♭ D♭	E G♯ B♯ (C)	E G♯ B D♯	E G B D
F	F A C	F A♭ C	F A C E♭	F A♭ C♭ E♭♭ (B) (D)	F A C♯	F A C E	F A♭ C E♭
F♯	F♯ A♯ C♯	F♯ A C♯	F♯ A♯ C♯ E	F♯ A C E♭	F♯ A♯ C𝄪 (D)	F♯ A♯ C♯ E♯ (F)	F♯ A C♯ E
G	G B D	G B♭ D	G B D F	G B♭ D♭ F♭ (E)	G B D♯	G B D F♯	G B♭ D F
A♭	A♭ C E♭	A♭ C♭ E♭ (B)	A♭ C E♭ G♭	A♭ C♭ E♭♭ G♭♭ (B) (D) (F)	A♭ C E	A♭ C E♭ G	A♭ C♭ E♭ G♭ (B)

ENHARMONIC SPELLING OF NOTES: Each key on the keyboard may be given more than one name. For example, C♯ is also named D♭. In spelling chords, the DOUBLE FLAT (♭♭) and the DOUBLE SHARP (𝄪) are often used. This is because chord spellings are easier to memorize using them. All of the above chords, properly spelled, skip one letter of the musical alphabet between each note. To change a major chord into an augmented chord, you simply raise the 5th of the chord one half-step. When a sharp is raised a half-step, it becomes a double sharp. Notice that the B augmented chord is spelled B D♯ F𝄪. The G in parentheses below the F𝄪 shows that F𝄪 is actually the same note as G. The notes F𝄪 and G are said to be ENHARMONIC. Similarly, a B♭♭ is the same note as A, as you will notice in the C diminished chord above.